Patterns of

Scientific Research

A Comparative Analysis of Research in Three Scientific Fields

by

Lowell L. Hargens

Indiana University

The Arnold and Caroline Rose Monograph Series of the American Sociological Association

ASA ROSE MONOGRAPH SERIES

Other publications in this series

Deviance, Selves and Others, Michael Schwartz and Sheldon Stryker (1971)

Socioeconomic Background and Educational Performance, Robert Mason Hauser (1972)

Black and White Self-Esteem: The Urban School Child, Morris Rosenberg and Roberta G. Simmons (1972)

Looking Ahead: Self-conceptions, Race and Family as Determinants of Adolescent Orientation to Achievement, Cad Gordon (1972)

Black Students in Protest: A Study of the Origins of the Black Student Movement, Anthony M. Orum (1972)

Attitudes and Facilitation in the Attainment of Status, Ruth M. Gasson, Archibald O. Haller, William H. Sewell (1972)

Patterns of Contact with Relatives, Sheila R. Klatzky (1972)

Interorganizational Activation in Urban Communities: Deductions from the Concept of System, Herman Turk (1973)

The Study of Political Commitment, John DeLameter (1973)

Ambition and Attainment, A Study of Four Samples of American Boys, Alan C. Kerckhoff (1974)

The Greek Peasant, Scott G. McNall (1974)

Available from the American Sociological Association, 1722 N Street, N.W., Washington, D.C. 20036.

Pre-paid costs: Members, $2.75 per title
Non-members, $5.00 per title
Complete Set, 20% discount

THE ARNOLD AND CAROLINE ROSE
MONOGRAPH SERIES IN SOCIOLOGY

A gift by Arnold and Caroline Rose to the American Sociological Association in 1968 provided for the establishment of the Arnold and Caroline Rose Monograph Series in Sociology. The conveyance provided for the publication of manuscripts in any subject matter field of sociology. The donors intended the series for rather short monographs, contributions that normally are beyond the scope of publication in regular academic journals.

The Series is under the general direction of an editorial board appointed by the Council of the American Sociological Association and responsible to the Publications Committee of the Association. Competition for publication in the Series has been limited by the Association to Members and Student Members.

Arnold Rose was my teacher and my friend. I was fully aware, before his untimely death, of his sense that sociology needed a publication outlet of the sort provided by this Series; and I was dimly aware of his hope that his and Caroline's gift would meet that need. I am grateful to the American Sociological Association for providing me the opportunity to help fulfill Arnold's hope.

Sheldon Stryker
Editor

January, 1975
Library of Congress Number 74-325-43
International Standard Book Number 0-912764-11-2

TABLE OF CONTENTS

LIST OF TABLES

LIST OF FIGURES

ACKNOWLEDGEMENTS

This monograph is a revision of sections of my doctoral dissertation, and I am especially grateful for the support I received from two of my teachers at the University of Wisconsin. David Mechanic first suggested that I carry out a study of researchers' reactions to difficulty in work, and generously provided the funds needed for the surveys reported here even though he originally envisioned a somewhat different study. The funds he provided came from the National Institute of Mental Health under grant number 5RO-MH14835. Warren O. Hagstrom provided instruction, advice, and encouragement through all of the stages of the study, and those acquainted with his work in the sociology of science and the sociology of work will recognize the substantial intellectual debts I owe him.

In addition, I received valuable comments on substantive and stylistic matters from Barbara F. Reskin, Clarence C. Schrag, William H. Sewell, and an anonymous reviewer for the monograph series. Helen MacGill Hughes copy-edited the entire manuscript and greatly increased its clarity and precision. My study obviously would have been impossible without the good will and patience of my respondents, and I would like to take this opportunity to thank them for their assistance.

Finally, I wish to thank Roy G. Francis for introducing me to the sociology of knowledge and science.

CHAPTER ONE

INTRODUCTION

This is a study of differences between disciplines in scientific research. It attempts to outline some of the linkages between the social organization of a scientific field and the personal experiences at work of those who work in it. Thus it is an essay on the more general sociological question of the relationships between social structure and personal experience.

The study focuses on the research activity and experience of samples of American academic scientists. They almost always are free to select their problems, methods and instruments, and to evaluate their findings. These freedoms in turn imply that academic scientists have power to control the setting and pace of their research. Research in academic settings is to be contrasted in these respects with most forms of industrial work wherein individual workers cannot freely choose objects and tools, bear little responsibility for evaluating outcomes and control neither the setting nor the pace of their endeavors.

The unique features of academic research offer several advantages and opportunities to a study of relationships between the social structure of work and the personal experience of workers. Academic scientists enjoy a high degree of autonomy in collectively controlling the social mechanisms which define the goals and means of their work and which allocate rewards for its successful performance. As a result, the social solidarity of a group of scientists may be expected to be more intimately related to their experience at work than is the case of other categories of workers. Being able to control the setting and pace of research also means that they exhibit a wider variety of work patterns, work-related difficulties and frustrations, and adaptive strategies for dealing with them, than do others. Since modern techniques and patterns of authority tend to standardize work behavior and experience, studies of scientific research have access to a much greater range of variation in these matters than is true of studies of other forms of work. Finally, academic scientists exhibit profound self-investment in their research. Their low level of alienation makes them especially liable to the exhilaration and frustration that attend the conditions of research. As a result, the effects of various characteristics of work on workers' experience may be expected to be more apparent among them than among more alienated workers.

In addition to its concern with the sociology of work, the investigation reported here is also a study in the sociology of science. Insofar as experience in scientific research is intimately connected to the social structure of scientific fields, research work is a strategic site for the study of the social structure of science.

To date, most work has been directed to the specification and explanation of characteristics of science taken as a whole, rather than to the determination of variation among scientific fields.[1] For example, two dominant research traditions in the sociology of science have been, first, attempts to specify the distinctive characteristics which differentiate science from other social institutions, and the social conditions under which the institution of science emerges and flourishes (Parsons, 1951; 332-334; Merton 1957a: 552-561; Barber, 1962: 122-142), and second, attempts to demonstrate the importance of general social and psychological processes in scientific endeavors (Merton, 1957b; Hagstrom, 1965; Storer, 1966). Research in these two traditions has tended to neglect variation between scientific fields; the first because of its concentration on science as a general social institution, the second because of its concentration on the motivation and social control of the individual scientist. Although it is not clear that the study of variation in patterns of research between fields will necessarily yield further information about either the distinctive characteristics of science or the general behavioral principles underlying it, it can be expected to yield clues about the links between the institutional and behavioral levels of contemporary science.

This is primarily an exploratory study whose data come from a variety of sources, including unstructured interviews with scientists, sample surveys of scientists in three disciplines, and secondary analyses of data from previously reported studies.

In the first stage of the study I interviewed 23 scientists who were at that time faculty members of the University of Wisconsin. Questions focused on general research practices, difficulties and frustrations encountered in research, and adaptive strategies employed to overcome them. Scientists in the departments of mathematics, physics, chemistry, and biochemistry were interviewed for from one-half to one and one-half hours. The interviews were conducted primarily to generate questions and hypotheses for further investigation, but comments made by the subjects are quoted at various points below. Data from these interviews, however, are not incorporated in any of the tabulations.

---

[1] A summary of the exceptions to this generalization will be found in Storer (1972: 229-268).

2

On the basis of the interviews and consultation with interested colleagues (who were also, at that time, my teachers), I developed a short questionnaire which included a variety of questions concerning scientific research practices and experiences. Its purpose was to obtain estimates of the importance of the research practices and experiences in each of several fields. At this point it was decided that the study would be focused on academic scientists at American universities, a restriction which has three advantages: First, basic scientific research is most highly concentrated in these institutions, and studies restricted to them will have relatively small dross rates resulting from the sampling of individuals who do not carry on research, or whose work is directed by superordinates (Hagstrom, 1965: 35-39). Second, confining the study to scientists with a single, relatively homogeneous type of employer eliminates one possible alternative explanation of observed differences between scientific fields. Third, adequate sampling rosters are more likely to be available to scientists at graduate institutions than to those employed elsewhere.

The decision as to which scientific fields to include in the study was based on a combination of theoretical and pragmatic considerations. Since this is primarily an exploratory study, it would be advantageous to select fields intentionally which are likely to show large differences in patterns of research, rather than to attempt to draw some type of probability sample of all scientific fields. In addition, samples large enough (200-300 cases) to support rudimentary multivariate analyses with a degree of statistical reliability were desired for each field. On the basis of these considerations it was decided to include a field from the physical sciences, one from the formal sciences, and one from the social sciences. The selection of particular fields from each of the three was based, first of all, on the criterion that within a chosen field there should be no great differences among specialties in terms of the kinds of instruments used in research and the typical patterns of its organization. For example, on the basis of this criterion, physics, which is probably the field most often studied by sociologists of science, was eliminated from consideration. Physics is actually fairly atypical in the extent of differentiation between theoretical and experimental work, and this differentiation is associated with large differences among specialties in the use of research instruments and in the degree to which collaboration is formally organized (Hagstrom, 1967; Gaston, 1973: 26-31). The second important criterion was the availability of a sampling roster of academic scientists. Of the physical sciences, chemistry was selected since it possessed the best directory of workers in graduate institutions. Of the social sciences, political science had the most recent directory and therefore it was included. None of the formal sciences possessed similar directories of members, and mathematics was selected because it is the largest of these fields. Systematic random samples of members of American university faculties in each of the three fields were then drawn. (A more detailed discussion of sampling rosters and procedures, as well as evidence of the representativeness of the sample is in the Appendix.)

Despite the fact that the use of information from sample surveys such as those carried out for this study is usually thought more appropriate to the testing of hypotheses than to their construction, in actual practice the latter tends to be predominant. Survey analysts are usually more interested in the interpretation and elaboration of empirical findings than in the testing of pre-specified hypotheses (Selvin and Stuart, 1966). This is also true of my use of the data obtained from the surveys of the research practices of chemists, mathematicians and political scientists. In order not to foster illusions on this point, I have not reported measures of the level of statistical significance for the various tabulations.[2] On the other hand, enough information is presented in each table to allow readers to make their own assessment of the statistical reliability of the results.

The final source of data for this study was a survey of mathematicians, chemists, physicists and biologists who were graduate faculty members at American universities in 1966. This survey was carried out by Warren O. Hagstrom in order to obtain information concerning competition for priority and patterns of organization of research in various scientific fields (1967: 98-129). The survey involved questionnaires mailed to sample respondents, telephone interviews with those who did not return questionnaires, and the collection of information from published directories and compilations such as *Science Citation Index*. Through the kindness of Professor Hagstrom, I was given the opportunity to carry out secondary analyses of these data, and tables from these analyses are presented in the following chapters.

The following pages contain discussion of three main topics, with a chapter devoted to each. In Chapter II a Durkheimian model of social integration in scientific disciplines is presented. Using evidence from this and previous studies, I argue that disciplines can be distinguished in terms of their relative "normative" and "functional" integration (these dimensions parallel Durkheim's concepts of "mechanical" and "organic" solidarity). Data concerning scientists' research experiences are employed both to support the argument and to suggest implications of the disciplines' social structures for experience at work.

Differences between disciplines in degree of routine in research are examined in Chapter III. Data concerning such topics as the planning and efficiency of work, the application of the division of labor to research, and the segregation of work from other spheres of life, are examined in this chapter. Scientists' reactions to routine are also examined. It is shown, for example, that routine in different disciplines is positively associated with strategies to lessen the debilitating effects of difficulties, and with avoidance of becoming personally upset or depressed by interruption or lack of progress.

In Chapter IV I examine arguments to account for the relative routine of research in scientific fields. Possible explanatory factors discussed here include the social integration of scientific fields, and the impact of new techniques on the organization of scientific research.

---

[2]An exception to this rule is made for reports of the results of multiple regression analyses because one cannot assess their reliability simply on the basis of the number of cases upon which they are carried out.

CHAPTER 2

SOCIAL SOLIDARITY IN SCIENTIFIC DISCIPLINES

Social theorists have repeatedly attempted to specify dimensions of variation in the strength of social bonds, and to construct concepts which may be generally applied to the whole range of human association. Although there is no preeminent solution to the problem of social integration, since Durkheim's *The Division of Labor In Society* sociologists have commonly distinguished between two possible bases of it. On the one hand, the members of a collectivity may be integrated through the mutual sharing of a body of beliefs and values.[1] This is Durkheim's "mechanical solidarity"—"the totality of beliefs and sentiments common to average citizens in the same society." On the other hand, they may be integrated through the interdependence of specialized individual activities or functions. This is his "organic solidarity"; it is analogous to the form of integration found between the organs of living bodies (1947:79, 353-354). In the following analysis, I will refer to them, respectively, as "normative integration" and "functional integration" (Landecker, 1951).

Durkheim's distinction has been made the framework of the following discussion because analyses of scientific activities are cast predominantly in terms of one or the other of his two modes of social integration. For example, those who view science as a unique activity tend to characterize it in terms of some normative configuration, the exact elements of which, however, vary from author to author. Philosophers of science have attempted to characterize science in terms of a set of criteria which may be used to distinguish scientific knowledge from other forms of knowledge (Feigl, 1953;

---

[1]The term "mutual sharing" is not redundant. The fact of sharing the same body of beliefs and values may not be as important as the mutual recognition of it. (Scheff, 1967).

Hempel, 1965), while sociologists characterize science as a social institution (Merton, 1957a; 550-561; Barber, 1962: 122-142; Storer, 1966: 75-90). However, these characterizations of scientific activity in terms of beliefs and values do not confront specifically the problem of determining variations in normative integration among scientific disciplines. The philosophers of science have been interested in discovering what normative elements should be used as criteria in judging *all* scientific knowledge rather than in how the criteria are met in various disciplines. Similarly, Merton attacks the problem of specifying the compatibility between the social norms which characterize *all* of science and the normative systems of entire societies. In contrast this chapter investigates the relative normative integration of specific scientific disciplines at given times.

In recent years sociologists of science have paid increasing attention to the study of scientific disciplines as functionally integrated systems. Indeed, their most recent work has been organized around exchange perspectives, which emphasize the social networks through which colleagues reward each other's scientific contributions (Merton, 1957b, 1965; Hagstrom, 1965; Storer, 1966). Questions of congruence of formal rewards and scientific contributions have been investigated in several scientific disciplines (Crane, 1965; Cole and Cole, 1967, 1968; Hargens and Hagstrom, 1967), as has the sociometric structure of diverse scientific groups (Price 1965a, Chapter 3, 1965b; Mullins, 1969; Crane, 1972). Unfortunately, these investigations usually have been analyses of a single discipline, even of a single specialty within a given discipline, rather than systematic comparisons of disciplines. Thus investigation of the relative functional integration of scientific disciplines will also be a major topic of this chapter.

Although distinctions between these two types of social integration have a long tradition, and although science has often been studied in terms of one or the other of the two poles of the distinction, there has been only one attempt to determine the possible consequences of the differential prevalence of each type of integration in scientific disciplines. In his discussion of anomie in science, Hagstrom (1964; 1965: 226-236) applied Durkheim's formulation of social integration in order to arrive at answers to these questions. In the following pages, I attempt to elaborate and extend Hagstrom's work.

Problems in Measuring Social Integration in Scientific Disciplines

Like many concepts in sociology, the ideas of normative and functional integration do not clearly imply appropriate measures. According to Durkheim,

. . . social solidarity is a completely moral phenomenon which, taken by itself, does not lend itself to exact observation nor indeed to measurement. To proceed to this classification and this comparison [of types of social solidarity], we must substitute for this internal fact which escapes us an external index which symbolizes it and study the former in terms of the latter (1947:64).

Unfortunately, the substitution he proposes of external indices for internal facts can be a perilous enterprise. Because a given concept usually cannot be indexed by a single observable characteristic, and because the latter often

6

indexes several theoretically distinguishable concepts, sociologists commonly disagree on the appropriateness of a specific measure or set of measures. In such a situation the safest strategy is to employ as many measures of a concept as possible and to be as suspicious of their reliability and validity as one usually is of the hypotheses of relations between the concepts. (Webb, et al., 1966).

Normative Integration

In this study, I attempt to determine the degree to which members of a discipline concur on the norms, values, and beliefs central to research in their discipline; I am not concerned with whether the norms, values and beliefs are consistent with each other (Landecker, 1951: 333-335). Thus if the members of a discipline interpret their research in terms of a common theoretical framework, I would judge that discipline to have a relatively high degree of normative integration despite the fact that the theory might contain logically inconsistent assumptions and postulates. In short, I am concerned with the social rather than the logical aspect of normative integration. Moreover, I am not concerned with the degree to which scientists in a given discipline subscribe to a higher order of "norms and values of science," such as Feigl's "intersubjective testability" or Merton's "universalism." These are perhaps fundamental norms and values without which institutionalized science is impossible, but they are scarcely sufficient for the initiation and maintenance of agreement about the questions, techniques and interpretations of scientific research.

Given these stipulations, one must consider two important obstacles to measuring a discipline's normative integration by obtaining information about its members' endorsement of various norms and values. First, it probably is impossible to specify all, or even a significant proportion of the norms and values involved in any kind of social activity, including science (Garfinkel, 1964; Kuhn, 1964: 43-51). But even were this possible, it would be prohibitive to list the norms and values, inquire about individuals' allegiances to each of them, and to construct some sort of overall index of the degree of integration of their allegiances. Second, it is clear that the distinction between "the truth" and "what is believed to be true" is particularly relevant to studies of normative integration. Indeed, to Scheff, (1967) normative integration is not so much a question of a population's agreement or disagreement on particular norms and values as of that population's understanding or misunderstanding of the extent of agreement. For example, members of a scientific discipline may be able to maintain a line of inquiry for a time because they *believe* that they agree on the meaning of their concepts and on the types of instruments appropriate to their research, even though in fact they may disagree about these points (Kuhn, 1964: 43-44). Scheff recommends, therefore, that perceptions of, as well as actual agreement or disagreement be investigated in research on normative systems.

These difficulties appear to rule out the possibility of obtaining overall measures of the normative integration in a scientific discipline by obtaining information about individual scientists' allegiance to the particular norms and values involved in their research. It is still possible, however, to obtain information relevant to normative integration by asking scientists to make reports about their perception of how far they agree on the general normative characteristics of their disciplines. For example, the perceived agreement among scientists in a particular field on the validity of published work in it may serve as an indicator of their perceived consensus on the rules and standards governing their research. Similarly, to the extent that scientists in a given field share a common theoretical perspective, they also concur on the importance of a set of relevant research questions (Kuhn, 1964: 35-44).

It is clear that this strategy yields information only about how far scientists *believe* that they have attained consensus, and that additional information is required to determine if they are right. I will argue that certain characteristics of the publishing of research work in a given field may be used to measure its normative integration independently of the perceptions of integration entertained by the given scientists. In this way it may be possible to assess the probability that the members of a discipline labor under a misunderstanding of their consensus on rules and standards.

Functional Integration

A functionally malintegrated (anomic) collectivity is one in which the specialized contributions of constituent units are not complementary. Many of Durkheim's examples of this condition involved economic systems; he asserted, for example, that when producers do not understand the interdependence of their market, the economic system ceases to function smoothly and economic crises result (Durkheim, 1947:369-370). Durkheim also pointed to the state of the social sciences of his time as another example of anomie:

> It is hardly a century since this new field of phenomena has been opened to scientific investigation. Scholars have installed themselves in them, some here, some there, according to their tastes. Scattered over this wide surface, they have remained until the present too remote from one another to feel all the ties which unite them (1947: 370).

Durkheim took pains to explain that anomie is not a normative phenomenon; thus to his mind attempts to strengthen the collective consciousness of an anomic community would not ameliorate the condition (1947:373-373). On the other hand, it is difficult to interpret phrases like "feel all the ties which unite them" in strictly non-normative terms. Indeed, most discussions of anomie have assumed at least implicitly that it is inversely related to normative integration.[2]

Hagstrom, in his discussion of anomie in science, also assumes that functional malintegration is associated with normative malintegration. According to him, members of anomic scientific communities are not aware of who is working on similar research problems or who will be affected by the solution of one's own problems.

---

[2]Durkheim (1947: 152-173) makes this argument, but he also qualifies it by suggesting that both mechanical and organic solidarity are always present to some degree and that no collectivity can be integrated in terms of only one. (Durkheim, 1974: 226-229).

The solidarity of a scientific community is normally maintained by the felt interdependence of specialized scientists who contribute information to one another and receive in exchange the recognition of their colleagues . . . Scientific anomy can be specified as the loss of solidarity following a general breakdown in the exchange of information and recognition . . . .

Communities are made anomic in a variety of ways; the common element seems to be a "declassification," which casts persons into social roles and statuses in which their customary relations with others are broken and the *standards formerly governing their behavior are no longer applicable* (1964: 186-187, 189; emphasis added).

After shifting his emphasis to anomie as a state of normlessness, Hagstrom proceeds to apply Merton's normative typology of social deviance (Merton, 1957a: 131-160) to behavior in scientific communities. He also employs indicators of anomie—such as how often published papers in a given field are evaluated as trivial—which appear to be as much a function of normative as of functional integration.

In the following discussion I avoid the assumption that low levels of functional integration are associated with low levels of normative integration, but rather I attempt to demonstrate that mathematics, relative to other fields, exhibits a low level of functional integration and at the same time a high level of normative integration. To do so it is necessary to choose indicators of functional malintegration which are not as sensitive to levels of normative integration as the indicators used by Hagstrom. In following sections, therefore, a variety of measures are presented to assess the functional integration in a field independent of its normative integration.

Normative and Functional Integration in Three Disciplines

One may locate scientific disciplines in terms of the space formed by the two dimensions of social integration discussed above. For example, Figure 2-1

Figure 2-1

Normative and Functional Integration in Mathematics, Chemistry and Political Science

Functional Integration	Normative Integration	
	High	Low
High	Chemistry	Political Science
Low	Mathematics	***

***Empty Cell

9

presents the relative locations of the three disciplines chosen, as indicated in Chapter One, to represent a formal science, a physical science, and a social science. The theoretical rationale for including a representative of each is indicated in Figure 2-1 by the arraying of the three disciplines in three cells,[3] the relative positions being hypothetical at this point.

Discussions of the differences between the social sciences and the natural sciences are focused predominantly upon the former's comparative lack of normative integration. Social scientists do not agree on what is known, and this circumstance is a fundamental element in distinctions between "hard" and "soft" sciences (Kuhn, 1964:164-165; Klaw, 1968:273-277). Thus in Figure 2-1 political science is represented as ranking low in normative integration, relative to mathematics and chemistry. It should be pointed out, however, that the sources of the normative integration in mathematics may be different from those in chemistry. As a formal science, mathematics involves paradigms whose features (rules for the solution of a problem and standards for determining when it had been reached, etc.) concern theoretical formulations not accessible to empirical proof. This circumstance may be associated with differential rates of paradigm succession between mathematics and the empirical sciences (Bochner, 1963) and may also be a feature which makes the existence of a high degree of normative integration possible in mathematics even in the presence of a low degree of functional integration.

Hagstrom and Fisher have presented anecdotal evidence to support the hypothesis of less functional integration in mathematics than in either the physical or the social sciences (Hagstrom, 1964; Fisher, 1973). Setting aside for the moment the question of its empirical truth, it should be noted that this hypothesis appears to contradict elements of Durkheim's original discussion of organic solidarity. Durkheim and most subsequent writers stipulate that the state of organic solidarity presupposes the existence of high specialization (Landecker, 1951: 338). Hagstrom, on the other, hand, states that a collectivity may be functionally integrated even though relatively unspecialized. For example, comparing anomie in mathematics and sociology, he says:

> Sociologists are not as highly specialized as mathematicians or most hard scientists: they find it relatively easy to acquire new techniques or to begin research in new substantive areas. At the same time "specialties" consisting of those engaged in research on similar topics are easily recognized, and most sociologists can probably identify many others who share their problems and compete with them in providing solutions. (1964:194)

Thus the concept of functional integration, as used here, is apparently

---

[3]Although the lower left-hand cell in Figure 2-1 is empty, it should not be assumed that disciplines with little normative and functional integration cannot be characterized as sciences. Figure 2-1 is a cross-sectional presentation of the positions of the three disciplines under study and it is clear that disciplines may move around in its two-dimensional space with the passage of time. Thus, Kuhn's discussion of the "crisis" stage which mediates the transition of a discipline from one paradigm to another would seem to be characterized by little normative and functional integration (Kuhn, 1964: 77-90).

incommensurate with Durkheim's concept of organic solidarity. This can also be shown in a diagram constructed on his dimensions:

Figure 2-2 indicates the conditions of specialization, normative integration, and functional integration characterizing societies which, in Durkheim's view, exhibit organic solidarity, mechanical solidarity, and anomie, in their most developed forms. One immediately notes that Durkheim's three ideal types compose only a subset of all the possible values which might fill the empty cells. [4] This circumstance is not surprising since Durkheim has been extensively criticised for his concepts' inadequacy in delineating the full range of possible states of social solidarity (Merton, 1934: 324-325). His failure may be attributed to his acceptance of a false evolutionary theory which minimized both the specialization present in normatively integrated primitive societies and the normative integration present in modern complex societies (Nisbet, 1965: 36-37). The incomplete nature of Durkheim's theory of social solidarity is also responsible for Hagstrom's inability to apply Durkheim's ideal types, in a strict fashion, to the analysis of social solidarity in scientific fields—as may be demonstrated by hypothetically locating the three disciplines in the framework employed in Figure 2-2:

Figure 2-2

**Relations of Specialization, Normative Integration
and Functional Integration with
Organic Solidarity, Mechanical Solidarity and Anomie**

	Specialization			
	High *Normative Integration*		Low *Normative Integration*	
	High	Low	High	Low
Functional Integration				
High	***	Organic Solidarity	***	***
Low	***	Anomie	Mechanical Solidarity	***

***Empty Cell

Although Figures 2-2 and 2-3 are not strictly comparable because the dimensions of the former are expressed in absolute terms while those of the latter

---

[4]Durkheim's other "abnormal" forms of the division of labor, the "forced division of labor" and "another abnormal form," involve the appropriateness of a collectivity's specialization rather than extent of its specialization and functional integration (Durkheim, 1947:374-395).

are comparisons among scientific fields, they may be combined insofar as one is willing to speak of *relative degrees* of, for example, organic solidarity in different fields. Superimposition of the one figure on the other reveals that none of the three fields occupy cells which correspond to any of Durkheim's three ideal types. Neither chemistry nor political science, both of which are hypothesized in Figure 2-3 as having relatively high degrees of functional

Figure 2-3

Specialization, Normative Integration and Functional Integration in Mathematics, Chemistry, and Political Science

	Specialization			
	High *Normative Integration*		Low *Normative Integration*	
	High	Low	High	Low
Functional Integration				
High	Chemistry	***	***	Political Science
Low	Mathematics	***	***	***

***Empty Cell

integration compared to mathematics, can be strictly characterized as exhibiting organic solidarity. This is because a high rather than low degree of normative integration is hypothesized of chemistry, while a low rather than a high degree of specialization is hypothesized of political science.

As a consequence of these considerations, the concepts of specialization, normative integration, and functional integration will be used hereafter in preference to Durkheim's terms, mechanical and organic solidarity, which tend to confine attention to only two of the possible combinations of the values of the three underlying variables. Similarly, the concept of anomie will be extended by specifying it as a general lack of functional integration, regardless of concurrent specialization and normative integration. This respecification will insure that questions about the relations of functional and normative integration will be posed as explicitly empirical questions rather than as questions implicitly contained in the concept of anomie itself. Finally, a general lack of normative integration, regardless of concurrent specialization and functional integration, will be referred to (following Hagstrom's terminology) as a state of "dissensus" (Hagstrom, 1964: 194).

Given these terminological conventions and the hypothetical positions of the three fields under study, I will present evidence which simultaneously bears upon the validity of the hypothetical positions and further explicates the nature of the three dimensions which underlie them.

Measures of Specialization, Normative Integration, and Functional Integration

Specialization

Just as science as a whole is divided into social sub-units referred to as disciplines, disciplines themselves are divided into sub-units referred to as specialties. Specialties as units are characterized by a greater homogeneity of research work than exists in their parent disciplines, and it may be on various dimensions. For example, some specialties are defined in terms of particular substantive research questions, others in terms of the use of particular techniques. Regardless of the dimensions of specialization in a discipline, its degree of specialization is determined by the ease with which those working in one specialty can take up research in another. Scientists in a highly specialized field must invest a considerable amount of time in familiarizing themselves with a new literature and new techniques before they can enter productively a different specialty. Measuring the specialization in a particular discipline presents many problems (Hagstrom, 1967: 160) and at present there is no systematic information on its extent in various scientific disciplines.

The most obvious way of measuring specialization is implied when it is defined in terms of ease of movement from one specialty to another. This is to measure it in terms of the extent to which scientists in a discipline are able to carry on research in several specialties simultaneously. Thus disciplines in which scholars exhibit high rates of change in specialty,[5] or commonly carry on research in several specialties, would be characterized as relatively unspecialized. But here two important difficulties arise:

First, actual rates of change in specialty (and, similarly, actual extent of multi-specialty research) are probably highly dependent upon the prevalence of competition. For example, even if the barriers to entry are formidable, scholars in substantial numbers may move to a specialty if new and in a discipline already characterized by stiff competition in existing specialties. Thus the actual extent of change of specialty and multi-specialty research is probably dependent upon factors independent of the specialization in a given discipline.

Second, this line of reasoning assumes the existence of several specialties within the disciplines under study. Comparisons among disciplines, therefore require lists of specialties, commensurable from discipline to discipline. Unfortunately, it is difficult to construct rosters of specialties even without attempting to make them commensurable (Hagstrom, 1967:71-75).

---

[5]Measures of rates of specialty change would have to take into account the fact that disciplines may vary in number of specialties: disciplines with many specialties tend to show higher rates of migration between specialties than those with a few broadly defined specialties. This problem is formally similar to that of comparing rates of migration within areal units (see Duncan, Cuzzort, and Duncan, 1961: 34).

In view of these difficulties, attempts to measure the specialization of a discipline must, it appears, be based upon the hypothetical character of the definition of specialization offered above, and must not presuppose the existence of lists of specialties by discipline. These are not impossible restrictions. For example, since ease of movement between specialties is determined by the extent to which the scholars in a discipline share research techniques and substantive information, specialization might be measured in these terms. As Kuhn (1964:23-25) points out, the most powerful impetus to the development of highly specialized and detailed information is commitment to a paradigm, and specialization is therefore limited by the normative consensus in a scientific discipline.[6] Kuhn's comparison of typical patterns of education in the natural and social sciences illustrates how deeply and continually students in the social sciences are made aware of the general theoretical debates in their disciplines, while, on the other hand, students in the natural sciences are given a shorter "theoretical" education through texts and then are encouraged to obtain more specialized knowledge and techniques by actually doing research:

> [In the social sciences] the elementary college course employs parallel readings in original sources, some of them the "classics" of the field, others the contemporary research reports that practitioners write for each other. As a result the student in any one of these disciplines is constantly made aware of the immense variety of problems that the members in his future group have, in the course of time, attempted to solve. Even more important, he constantly has before him a number of competing and incommensurable solutions to these problems, solutions that he must ultimately evaluate for himself.

> Contrast this situation with that in at least the contemporary natural sciences. In these fields the student relies mainly on textbooks until, in his third or fourth year of graduate work, he begins his own research. Many science curricula do not ask even graduate students to read in works not written specially for students (1964:164).

Thus, while graduate students in the natural sciences are obtaining the specialized information they need to carry on research, those in the social sciences are continually exposed to general theoretical issues and debates, and to general courses in method applicable to entire disciplines. Whereas students in the social sciences typically learn in these general courses the research techniques they will use later, graduate students in the natural sciences typically learn the techniques they will use in the course of doing research.

Differential levels of specialization between disciplines may also be related to differential levels of training required for adequate performance in research. In general, one may expect greater specialization to require longer training. This does not imply that training may be used as an accurate indicator of

---

[6]This hypothesis might be represented in Figure 2-2 by placing zeros in the cells, denoting a high degree of specialization where normative integration is low (i.e., the "organic solidarity" and "anomie" cells). Sociologists of science have stressed the importance of competition as the process by which normative consensus and specialization are linked (Collins, 1968).

specialization, for, given a constant level of specialization, education in a given discipline will be positively related to the financial support available for further training, and negatively related to the scarcity of scholars in that discipline. On the other hand, given information about the last-named factors, one may be able to make inferences about degree of specialization on the basis of an indicator such as the proportion of a discipline's members who have done postdoctorate work.[7] In 1960 Berelson reported that of a sample of graduate faculty in the United States, 29% of those in the physical sciences (including mathematics) had had postdoctoral fellowships in contract to 13% in the social sciences. Berelson found, moreover, that 16% of the physical scientists in a sample of recent recipients of the doctorate, but only 9% of the social scientists, had had postdoctoral fellowships (1960:190). In my samples, 49% of the chemists, 28% of the mathematicians, and 25% of the political scientists had had postdoctoral fellowships. Although the difference between political science and mathematics is fairly small here, it should be remembered that, at the time of these surveys, the demand for new Ph.D.'s was higher in the latter than in the former (Brown, 1967:12-14). In addition, there is evidence that postdoctorate work is more necessary in mathematics and chemistry than in political science. Berelson stated that 62% of his sample of graduate faculty in the physical sciences believe this to be the case as opposed to 48% of his social scientists, and he cited a remark made by a leading mathematician:

> . . . in (mathematics) a student must master the earlier material as well as the new . . . the Ph.D. has, in effect, a general education in mathematics; he needs more specialization and that is where the postdoctoral program comes in (1960:191).

Thus chemists and mathematicians are more likely to have completed postdoctoral work than are political scientists, and this is true even in the face of greater labor shortages in the former two groups than in the latter. Furthermore, it is not clear that political scientists feel deprived of support in postdoctoral work. Indeed, the evidence suggests that they do not believe that his extra training is needed as much as it is in mathematics and chemistry.

If these arguments for the hypothesis that social scientists have not developed the specialized knowledge and specialized techniques which typically exist in the natural and physical sciences are valid, then social scientists should be able to comprehend the work of others in their disciplines more easily than those in the natural sciences can do the same in their own disciplines. This should be true because the greater specialization in the latter fields implies more diverse research techniques and more specialized information than in the social sciences. Data which may be interpreted as supporting evidence have been presented by Garvey, Lin and Nelson, who report that social scientists, even though they have less advance familiarity with research reports given at national meetings than do natural scientists, also make fewer attempts to remedy this situation before the meetings than do natural scientists (1970:72-76). When scientists throughout a discipline share research

---

[7]Another possible measure of length of training, the number of years of full-time study taken to earn the Ph.D., shows little variation from field to field (Berelson, 1960: 159; Wilson, 1965: 19-40). The relative incidence of postdoctoral work in diverse fields is apparently a more valid measure of length of training.

techniques and have not developed specialized information about their topics, one would expect them to be able to assimilate information presented in research reports more easily than when these conditions are not present.

As is apparent by now, very little empirical evidence directly supports my claim that there is less specialization in political science than in mathematics or chemistry. Further research on specialization in science may be expected not only to extend our information on pertinent forms of evidence to other disciplines and through time, but also to suggest additional forms of evidence. As it stands, the problem of measuring specialization in science continues to be one of the most important, and, at the same time, difficult tasks facing the sociology of science.

Normative Integration

I have suggested that two possibly different aspects of normative integration be investigated: agreement on the relative importance of research questions, and agreement on the validity of published work. Although most accounts of normative integration in science imply that these two aspects are very highly related and even form a single dimension, this assertion should be investigated as an empirical question. This is not to suggest that these two aspects of the concept of normative integration are exhaustive: rather, they have been chosen for this research because they appear to correspond to the traditional distinction between means and ends.

Table 2-1 presents the distribution of answers in my samples to a question on agreement on the relative importance of research questions in various fields. The findings are consistent with the hypothesis that mathematics and chemistry are more integrated normatively than is political science. Moreover, differences in the response patterns of chemists and mathematicians are fairly small compared to their respective deviations from the response pattern of political scientists.

Table 2-2 presents the distribution of answers of the members of my samples to a question on agreement about the validity of published work. Once again mathematicians and chemists claim more normative integration than do political scientists. In comparison to Table 2-1 however, chemists show a response pattern more similar to that of political scientists than of mathematicians. The difference between findings reported in Tables 2-1 and 2-2 in this respect is clearly portrayed in Table 2-3 which presents values of the Index of Dissimilarity of differences in the response patterns in each of the tables. The relative frequency of perceived consensus among the mathematicians in Table 2-2 may be attributable to the fact that, as a formal science, mathematics enjoys comparatively well-developed standards of proof. This is probably less true of the empirical sciences, even of those which, like chemistry, would otherwise be characterized as normatively highly integrated.

The difference between mathematicians' and chemists' response patterns in Tables 2-1 and 2-2 may serve as a warning against treating normative integration as a unitary trait. As far as the rankings of the three fields are concerned, however, both tables show relatively greater dissensus in political science than in the other two fields.

Table 2-1. Responses to the Question: "To what degree do men in your research field agree on the relative importance of various research questions in that field?", by Discipline

	Discipline		
Responses	Mathematics	Chemistry	Political Science
There is a high degree of agreement on the relative importance of all research questions	12%	3%	1%
There is agreement on a majority of research questions, but some disagreement exists over others	50	56	32
There is some agreement on the importance of a few major questions, but little agreement about the rest	32	33	47
There is little agreement on the relative importance of various research questions	6	8	19
	100%	100%	99%
N	(181)	(213)	(211)

The same result is shown by responses to a question about the prevalence of intellectual "schools" in the three disciplines. The existence of such schools is commonly interpreted as a clear indication of dissensus, whatever its basis. Table 2-4 presents patterns of response which are somewhat between those shown in Tables 2-1 and 2-2. The Index of Dissimilarity of the responses of chemists and mathematicians in table 2-4 is .24, while that of chemists and political scientists is .46 and of mathematicians and political scientists is .64. These values, when compared to those presented in Table 2-3, show chemists as relatively more unlike mathematicians in Table 2-4 than in Table 2-1, and relatively more unlike political scientists in Table 2-4 than in Table 2-2. The results presented in Table 2-4, then, justify the use of the scientists' perceptions of competing schools as an indicator of their perceptions of their fields' normative integration. As to the rankings of the three fields, the findings in Table 2-4 corroborate those in the previous tables.

So far the only evidence presented in support of the hypothesis of the greater normative integration of mathematics and chemistry has been derived

Table 2-2. Responses to the Question: "To what extent is there disagreement among men in your research field over the validity of published answers to research questions in that area?", by Discipline

	Discipline		
Responses	Mathematics	Chemistry	Political Science
Such disagreement almost never exists	66%	5%	1%
Such disagreement sometimes exists, but it is fairly unusual	25	45	15
Such disagreement often exists	7	45	62
Such disagreement almost always exists	1	6	21
	99%	101%	99%
N	(181)	(215)	(210)

Table 2-3. Values of the Index of Dissimilarity* of Response Patterns

	Comparisons of Disciplines		
Response Patterns	Mathematics & Chemistry	Mathematics and Political Science	Chemistry and Political Science
Agreement on importance of various research questions (Table 2-1)	.09	.28	.26
Disagreement on validity of published answers to research questions (Table 2-2)	.62	.75	.33

*For a discussion of this index, see Taeuber and Taeuber (1965:28-30, 202-216).

18

Table 2-4. Responses to the Question: "Work on a particular research question sometimes becomes organized in terms of competing perspectives or 'schools'—How many research questions in your field have this characteristic?", by Discipline

	Discipline		
Responses	Mathematics	Chemistry	Political Science
There are no competing schools in my field	36%	12%	1%
Competing schools exist with respect to only a few research questions in my field	46	52	17
Competing schools exist with respect to many research questions in my field, but not with respect to others	14	31	50
This is a characteristic of all of the research questions in my field	4	5	32
	100%	100%	100%
N	(178)	(213)	(212)

Table 2-5. Rejection Rates of Journals in Selected Scientific Disciplines, 1967

Discipline	Mean Rejection Rate	Number of Journals
Physics	24%	12
Biological Sciences	29%	12
Chemistry	31%	5
Mathematics	44%	4
Economics	69%	4
Sociology	78%	14
Political Science	84%	2

from the scientists' perceptions of various facets of it in their respective fields. Let us now turn to forms of evidence which do not involve such perceptions. Although there are no direct objective measures of normative integration in scientific disciplines, it would appear that certain characteristics can be interpreted as indirect measures. For example, Zuckerman and Merton recently suggested that differences between disciplines in the rejection rates of their journals might reflect their relative normative integration (1971: 71-80). The argument implied is straightforward: When scientists agree on the identity and importance of various research questions in their field, and also 'on the strategies and techniques to investigate them, they will be able to produce research which is received as a contribution to knowledge. But when they do not agree on these standards, judgments that particular papers do not constitute contributions to knowledge will be more frequent and the rejection rates of their journals will be higher.

Table 2-5 reproduces some results reported by Zuckerman and Merton:[8] The relative rankings of disciplines shown in Table 2-5 confirm the expectation of lower rejection rates in the "hard" than in the "soft" sciences, except in mathematics. Before accepting mathematics' unexpectedly high rejection rate as positive evidence of the relative absence of normative integration, however, some common alternative explanations of variation in rejection rates among scientific disciplines should be noted. They usually focus upon the space limitations which hamper journal editors. In the short run at least, lack of space in the learned journals can result in higher than usual rejection rates and it might therefore be asked to what extent the results presented in Table 2-5 are a function of differential pressures on the journals' space.

Unfortunately, Zuckerman and Merton have not presented information about shortage of space in the journals of the fields they studied. Furthermore, in only four or five cases can their data be even roughly matched with data from the lists of disciplines used in published studies of shortages, notably those presented by the National Science Foundation's Office of Science Information Service (1964).[9] However, three of the cases are chemistry, mathematics and statistics, and an aggregate category containing various social sciences. Data on differential scarcity of space in these fields may possibly shed light on their rejection rates.

Table 2-6 presents data for two possible measures of the scarcity of journal space. The first, a measure of the active research population in a field in

---

[8]In their published report, Zuckerman and Merton present an estimate of the rejection rate which characterizes an aggregate of mathematics and statistics journals. Zuckerman kindly furnished me with the estimate shown in Table 2-5 for mathematics journals alone.

[9]In addition, the most recent data presented in the N.S.F. study were collected for the year 1959 and antedate the Zuckerman-Merton data by eight years. A later survey of these topics was sponsored by the N.S.F. in 1962, and preliminary results were reported in the 1964 volume cited here. Although more recent data are not available, the stability in the relative rankings of various fields in the 1949, 1959 and 1962 studies of most available measures suggest that the relative differences shown below persisted during the period of the Zuckerman-Merton study.

Table 2-6. **Space Shortage in the Journals of Chemistry, Mathematics and Statistics, and the Social Sciences, 1959**

Indicator	Discipline		
	Chemistry	Mathematics & Statistics	Social Sciences
Ratio of mean circulation to mean number of articles published	22.0	50.1	51.6
Ratio of mean number of accepted articles in backlog to mean number of articles published	2.9	.50	.45

comparison to the amount of research actually published, consists of the ratio of the mean circulation of a discipline's journals to the mean number of articles they publish in a year.[10] The second measure provides an indication of possible space shortages as they are manifested in the actual operation of given learned journals. It is the ratio of the mean number of accepted articles which are in the backlogs of the disciplines' journals, to the mean number of articles they have published (National Science Foundation, 1964: 7-8).

Insofar as these measures are valid indicators,[11] Table 2-6 reveals that mathematics and the social sciences appear to experience greater shortages than does chemistry. It is notable, however, that the values for the social sciences are about the same as those for mathematics, even though the social sciences have much higher rejection rates than mathematics. It is therefore doubtful that differences in the rejection rates (Table 2-5), can be dismissed

---

[10]This ratio was computed from data presented in Tables 3 and 13 of the 1964 N.S.F. report.

[11]There is a good reason to suspect that these measures may reflect other characteristics of disciplines as well as space shortages. For instance, the more direct of the two measures, the ratio of the backlog to actually published articles, is probably more a function of competition in different fields than of space shortages. Supporting evidence may be found in the fairly frequent statements of editors of social science journals that they do *not* face an overabundance of publishable papers (Ryder, 1968; Mansfield, 1962). Thus it does not appear that the large backlogs which characterize the social sciences are a result of acute shortage of space. Later I will argue that backlogs are a good indication of competition; the greater the competition, the smaller the backlog. I have been unable to find statements similar to those cited above regarding the social sciences by editors of journals in mathematics. Indeed, few of the latter journals contain anything but research reports (no editorial comment, letters to editors, advertising, etc.). These findings are consistent with the conclusion reached below that mathematics journals may experience space shortages, but that this is not true of social science journals.

as a simple reflection of differential pressure on space. The results presented in Table 2-6 are consistent with the hypothesis that the higher rejection rates in mathematics in comparison with those in chemistry (Table 2-5), may be due to greater pressure on space in the former. It is also questionable, then, whether mathematics' higher rejection rate signalizes a lesser degree of normative integration than is to be found in chemistry.

Further support for this conclusion can be gained by examining another possible measure of normative integration: the average length of Ph.D. dissertations in the given field. One might expect, and the evidence confirms, that Ph.D. dissertations are longer in disciplines believed to be marked by a great deal of dissensus than in fields commonly thought highly integrated. Differences in average length of dissertation between one field and another would appear to be a function primarily of the relative extent of consensus on standards of proof from field to field. Where standards are not shared or are ambiguous, the establishment of a thesis requires more lengthy and elaborate argumentation than it does where standards are highly developed and agreed upon.

Berelson (1960: 181-182) has published data on the median length of dissertation for a list of disciplines which can to some extent be compared with that used by Zuckerman and Merton. Rather than presenting the simple distribution of median length of dissertation by discipline, I will show its joint distribution with the data on rejection rates presented by Zuckerman and Merton for comparable fields. This will make it possible not only to rank fields by the median lengths of dissertations, but also to learn how much the two possible measures of normative integration converge.

Figure 2-4 presents the scatter diagram for the association between the Zuckerman-Merton data on rejection rates and the Berelson data on median length of dissertation. Except in four fields—mathematics, psychology, geology and anthropology—they do appear fairly convergent.[12] Zuckerman and Merton have pointed out that two of the four deviant cases, psychology and anthropology, are composite fields which include some subfields akin to some of those in the physical sciences (e.g., physiological and experimental psychology, and physical anthropology) and others akin to some of those in the social sciences (e.g., clinical and social psychology, and cultural anthropology). If the data necessary to decompose these two fields into

---

[12]The comparability of these two sets of data is limited in two respects: First, Berelson's data were collected for the year 1957, a decade earlier than the Zuckerman-Merton data. It seems unlikely, however, that the relative ranking of the fields in terms of the average length of dissertation has changed appreciably since 1957. Second, Zuckerman and Merton present separate rejection rates for experimental and physiological psychology, on one hand (51%) and clinical, educational, abnormal, and social psychology, on the other (70%). Berelson, however, reports only one median length of dissertation in psychology. In Figure 2-4 I have arbitrarily chosen 60% as an estimate of the rejection rate in psychology as a whole. In general, Berelson's data on length of dissertation are probably statistically more reliable than the Zuckerman-Merton data on rejection rates. Insofar as both are valid measures of normative integration, inconsistencies between them are more likely to be due to unreliability in the rejection rates.

FIGURE 2-4

Mean Rejection Rates of Journals, and Median Length of Ph.D Dissertations for Selected Scientific Fields.

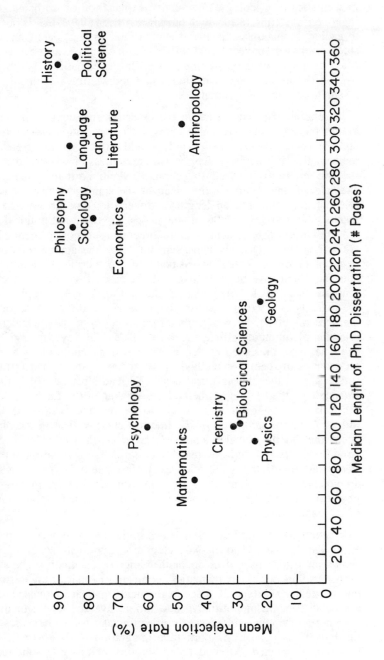

their subfields were available, the subfields would presumably lie closer to a line of best fit in Figure 2-4. The deviant cases, therefore, appear to be mathematics and geology. A tentative explanation of mathematics' surprisingly high rejection rate, which has already been suggested, is not applicable to geology's unexpectedly low rejection rate. In fact, data from the N.S.F. study discussed above suggest that the earth sciences, as a category, exhibit space shortages as great as those found in mathematics (1964:8,14); moreover, it should be noted that Zuckerman and Merton's estimate is based on a sample of only two journals.

In general, the data based on the objective measures of normative integration presented here are consistent with the expectation that political science and the social sciences as a whole would exhibit more dissensus than do mathematics or chemistry. This is true regardless of whether one or both of the two measures is used to estimate overall normative integration. For example, if one computes the mean of the standard scores of each field's rejection rate and median length of dissertation one obtains the following results: chemistry $= -1.06$, mathematics $= -.98$, and political science $= +1.26$. Unfortunately, data on more direct measures of normative integration are fragmentary. One such measure might be the amount of disagreement between journal referees' assessments of the merits of submitted articles, data for which have been published in the case of one or two social science journals (Seeman, 1966). However, data for reasonably complete samples of the journals of a variety of disciplines are not available. A second possible measure might be derived from information about the typical reasons for rejection of submitted articles in various fields. Garvey, Lin and Nelson, for example, have presented evidence that papers are more likely to be rejected on grounds of theory or method in the social sciences than in the physical sciences, and that this is true "despite" (read "because of") the fact that standards of theory and of method are weaker in the former fields. On the other hand, a paper is more likely to be rejected because the subject is judged to be inappropriate or the findings controversial in the physical sciences than in the social sciences (Garvey, *et al.* 1970:82-83). Both these conditions appear to indicate the greater normative integration of the physical as contrasted with the social sciences. Unfortunately Garvey, Lin and Nelson do not present this kind of information for specific disciplines within the physical and social sciences, and their study does not include mathematics or any other formal science.

In summary: Regardless of whether subjective or objective measures are employed to assess normative integration, political science consistently shows more dissensus than do mathematics or chemistry. The surprisingly high rejection rate of mathematics, compared to that of chemistry, may be due to greater shortage of space in the mathematical journals. Furthermore, a second measure of normative integration, average length of dissertation, does not confirm the evidence of the rejection rates for mathematics. Therefore the hypothesis concerning normative integration in the three fields may be tentatively accepted. More detailed scrutiny of possible subdimensions of normative integration, such as agreement on the relative importance of various research questions as opposed to agreement on appropriate techniques, and attempts to estimate false consensus and pluralistic ignorance call for the development of additional measures and their systematic application to diverse scientific disciplines.

Specialization and Normative Integration in Political Science

Political science, and the social sciences generally, may be characterized in terms of their *relative* lack of normative integration as compared with the natural and formal sciences. Moreover, observers sometimes report little absolute normative integration in the social sciences. Thus Spencer Klaw, in explaining why his book, *The New Brahmins,* does not discuss the social sciences, states:

> *Social scientists disagree violently about what they should be doing, and how they should be doing it.* If you ask a random selection of high-energy physicists to name the best people in their field, their answers will tend to agree, whereas in sociology, for example, you will get one list if you ask an admirer of the late C. Wright Mills and another if you ask a disciple of Talcott Parons (1968:273).

The determination of the absolute degree of normative integration in a given discipline is a very difficult problem. In gathering citation data for political scientists in my sample, however, I obtained evidence bearing on both this question and that of specialization in political science.

To the extent that a discipline is composed of highly developed specialties or organized in competing schools, the various journals in it might be expected to exhibit different patterns of citation. The assumption is that journals tend to differ in terms of the given discipline's specialties and/or schools. If this is the case, scholars extensively cited in one journal may not appear at all in another, and vice versa. The number of citations of each of the political scientists in my sample in a variety of political science journals yields evidence of the prevalence of this condition.[13] To this end I selected ten journals, some central to political science (for example, *American Political Science Review)* and others more peripheral (for example, *Foreign Affairs* and *Administrative Science Quarterly),* and computed the correlations between citation patterns from the 1968 issues of each of the ten, plus the 1967 issues of APSR.[14]

Table 2-7 presents the matrix of the intercorrelations. Except for those involving *Administrative Science Quarterly, Political Science Quarterly,* and *Foreign Affairs* they are fairly high, but to further summarize them they were

---

[13]The validity of this strategy depends upon the adequacy of the samples of men and journals. The sample of journals employed here is a purposive sample chosen so as to include journals reflecting various substantive and technical interests. A list of the journals included in the sample is presented in Table 2-7.

The validity of basing analyses on simple counts of citations is often challenged because not all citations are "positive." In my compilation of citation data of political scientists, however, I found that "negative" citations are extremely rare and can be discounted as a source of any nontrivial error in measurement.

[14]Using the 293 political scientists in my sample as observations, I computed the correlations between the numbers of citations to them appearing in each of the journals.

Table 2-7. Correlations Between Citation Patterns of Ten Journals Which Publish the Work of Political Scientists

	Mean No. of Citations per Individual	S.D.	1.	2.	3.	4.	5.	6.	7.	8.	9.	10.	11.
1. American Political Science Review (1967)	.56	2.44	—	.72	.38	.32	.39	.49	.63	.72	.65	.73	.51
2. American Political Science Review (1968)	.84	3.33		—	.58	.42	.12	.30	.72	.62	.72	.85	.76
3. Public Opinion Quarterly	.08	.41			—	.28	.09	.12	.54	.36	.38	.53	.60
4. Political Science Quarterly	.02	.22				—	.36	.24	.39	.32	.22	.29	.27
5. Foreign Affairs	.01	.08					—	.33	.30	.33	.14	.12	.04
6. Administrative Science Quarterly	.03	.25						—	.26	.47	.40	.32	.09
7. American Behavioral Scientist	.14	1.05							—	.65	.48	.56	.78
8. World Politics	.20	.96								—	.77	.73	.42
9. Comparative Political Studies	.31	2.51									—	.85	.32
10. Journal of Politics	.58	2.39										—	.58
11. Western Political Quarterly	.43	3.00											—

Table 2-8. Orthogonal Rotated Factors from Correlations between Citation Patterns of Political Science Journals

Journal	Factor I	Factor II	Factor III
1. American Political Science Review (1967)	.78	.10	.24
2. American Political Science Review (1968)	.92	−.04	−.09
3. Public Opinion Quarterly	.60	−.19	−.12
4. Political Science Quarterly	.39	−.12	.25
5. Foreign Affairs	.21	−.03	.53
6. Administrative Science Quarterly	.36	.21	.37
7. American Behavioral Scientist	.78	−.32	.14
8. World Politics	.76	.23	.26
9. Comparative Political Studies	.78	.46	.02
10. Journal of Politics	.88	.26	−.09
11. Western Political Quarterly	.75	−.45	−.16
% of Total Variance	.48	.07	.06

subjected to a factor analysis whose results are presented in Table 2-8.[15] The substantial single factor in Table 2-8 reflects a general correspondence in the patterns of citation of the journals. The three journals with the smallest loadings on the general factor are those which had the smallest correlations and standard deviations in Table 2-7. The *Administrative Science Quarterly* is a journal which emphasizes organizational analysis, featuring the work of scholars in business administration and sociology to a greater extent than the work of scholars in political science. *Foreign Affairs* is unique in featuring articles of a journalistic and/or normative nature with few, if any, citations of external literature; indeed, to the extent that a scientific journal is defined as a channel of formal scholarly recognition, *Foreign Affairs* could not be considered a scientific journal at all. Finally, the *Political Science Quarterly* specializes in articles by scholars engaged in various types of documentary

[15]An image analysis using S^2 estimates of uniqueness (Guttman, 1953) was carried out and the resulting factors were rotated by the quartimax method (Harmon, 1960: 294-311).

research who, in general, cite documents (governmental and news reports, the writings of classical political theorists, etc.) and not the work of their contemporaries. Thus the three journals contain few citations of the work of contemporary political scientists.

If it is valid to state that differentiation between disciplines gives rise to journals with different patterns of citation, the proffered evidence suggests that political science is not highly differentiated. To some extent this attests the relative lack of specialization in political science discussed earlier. But even in the absence of specialization, diverse patterns of citation would be found if work in political science were indeed organized in close-knit schools, as is popularly assumed. Thus there is evidence of a degree of normative consensus not usually acknowledged by critics of the social sciences.

Functional Integration

In this section I present evidence supporting the hypothesis that mathematics is functionally less integrated than is either chemistry or political science. Three kinds of evidence will be discussed: individual scientists' perceptions of their disciplines, behavior or adaptation on their part which ought to be consequences of a state of anomie, and characteristics of the disciplines themselves which should be associated with anomie.

The only previous research on anomie in science, that of Hagstrom (1964) relied heavily upon scientists' perceptions of various characteristics of their disciplines. This strategy faces two important difficulties. First, scientists are possibly mistaken about the existence or non-existence of various indicators anomie. Since demonstration of their perception of it is insufficient proof by itself, there must be supplementary evidence that the condition actually exists. Second, it is difficult to phrase understandable direct questions about the extent of complementarity and awareness of each other's work in their field. Questions designed to measure indirectly perceptions of functional integration often focus on characteristics which are affected by both normative and functional integration. In his most recent survey of scientists, however, Hagstrom obtained data which more clearly indicate functional integration by asking his respondents: "Have you ever found that another scientist has published results you published earlier, without referring to your work?" Of those who responded affirmatively to this question, 74% of the mathematicians and 59% of the chemists suggested that the other scientist probably did not know of the original work (1967: 127). Unfortunately, Hagstrom did not obtain information about political science or any other social science, but his results are consistent with the claim that mathematics suffers more anomie than does chemistry.

Most of the information I used to measure functional integration consists of data on behavior and adaptation which should be associated with anomie. For example, to the extent that scientists feel that their work has little import for the work of others (and vice versa), one would expect to find low rates of professional communication between them and their colleagues. I asked the scientists in my samples questions from which I computed the amount of time they spent on professional correspondence in a typical week; the results are reported in Table 2-9. Professional communication with colleagues is also

Table 2-9. Hours per Week Spent on Professional Correspondence, by Discipline

| | Discipline | | |
	Mathematics	Chemistry	Political Science
Mean	2.7	4.1	3.7
Standard Deviation	3.3	3.0	3.4
N	(167)	(212)	(200)

Table 2-10. Days Spent Last Year at Professional Meetings, Conferences, and Foundation or Governmental Agency Meetings, by Discipline

| Number of Days | Discipline | | |
	Mathematics	Chemistry	Political Science
0	11%	2%	0%
1- 5	35	35	24
6 10	28	33	36
11-20	16	21	26
21+	9	8	14
	99%	99%	100%
N	(179)	(218)	(212)

manifested in attendance at meetings and conferences of scientific associations, and participation in foundations or governmental agencies. Table 2-10 shows findings corroborating Table 2-9: that mathematicians engage less in professional communication than do chemists or political scientists.

Functional integration in a social system is related to the withdrawal of its productive members, suicide being the most spectacular mode (Durkheim, 1951:241-276). Hagstrom describes less extreme forms:

Failure to be recognized, to have one's own judgment reinforced by the judgments of others, may lead to a loss of faith in the value of one's own work. When a man is highly specialized, and especially when he is old and dislikes the idea of spending years working into a new specialty, such loss of faith may be followed by a general withdrawal from creative work, a renunciation of both the goals and means of science (1964: 192; see also Fisher, 1967).

Thus, if my earlier characterizations of the three disciplines are correct, mathematics should also be distinguished by higher rates of withdrawal than are chemistry and political science. Information collected for this study supports the conclusion: among the respondents in mathematics, 11% reported that they do not carry on research, while the proportions in both chemistry and political science were 3%.

Of course, these differences in proportion of scholars who do not carry on research are not necessarily the consequence of varied degrees of anomie, and alternative explanations could be imagined. Evidence is needed showing that mathematicians do, in fact, have less faith in the value of their own work—a condition implied by the hypothesis that mathematics is more anomic than the other fields. Some evidence is available in responses to a question I asked my respondents about the extent to which they sometimes feel their research problems are not very significant, and lose interest in them. Insofar as scientists find clues to the importance of their work in the formal and informal recognition of their colleagues, one would expect the incidence of this complaint to be positively related to anomie. Consistent with this expectation (and with the hypothesis that mathematics is more anomic than chemistry or political science), 12% of the mathematicians in my sample (N = 178) reported that this is often involved in the onset of their less productive periods, while among chemists (N = 218) and political scientists (N = 212) the proportions were 6% and 7%, respectively.

Thus far I have presented evidence that mathematicians are more likely than chemists or political scientists to regard their colleagues as unaware of their work, to engage less in professional communication and to tend toward long-run adaptations (withdrawal) or a sort most prevalent in anomic fields. These are all manifestations of anomie in a discipline which one would expect to find in individuals.

There are, however, other characteristics of scientific disciplines associated with their functional integration. One is competition for priority in presenting solutions to scientific problems. This kind of competition is affected by both the discipline's normative and its functional integration. If scholars agree on the nature of the "important" problems and on the general rules or techniques for solving them, then the extent to which they compete will be an indicator of the interrelatedness of their efforts.[16] Thus, given information about the normative integration in a number of disciplines, one may then make inferences about their relative functional integration from the prevalence of competition.

---

[16]This assumes that the maximally efficient organizational structure of science is that based upon competition between individuals and organizations. Although there has been much debate about this assumption (Polanyi, 1955), and although it has been demonstrated that the market imperfections typically present in *laissez faire* systems are also present in science (Hagstrom, 1965: 81-100), there is some evidence that the competitive model is more efficient than other forms of coordination (Ben-David, 1960).

Hagstrom has shown that chemists are more likely than mathematicians to perceive that they are involved in a competitive field. Table 2-11 reproduces data from his essay "Competition and Teamwork in Science" (1967:124-126) which demonstrate the point. Once again, there are no available data on a group of social scientists but, given the roughly similar extent of normative integration in mathematics and chemistry presented earlier, these data are consistent with the hypothesis that mathematics is less integrated functionally than is chemistry.

Table 2-11. **Mathematicians' and Chemists' Responses Regarding Competition**

	Discipline	
Percent respondents who:	**Mathematics**	**Chemistry**
1. Have never been antiicpated by others in the presentation of findings	46% (286)*	32% (516)
2. Are not concerned about being anticipated in present research	39 (283)	22 (518)
3. Feel safe in discussing current research with all others doing similar work at other institutions	56 (283)	36 (516)
4. Have not considered selecting problems in another specialty because of competition in their present areas	90 (196)	77 (427)

*Numbers in parentheses are numbers of cases on which percentages are based.

In order to measure the prevalence of competition in a discipline one may also examine the amount of time which typically elapses between the submission of papers to appropriate journals and their ultimate publication. In strongly competitive fields, the interval should be relatively short because there scholars are anxious to reduce the chance of their being anticipated by others (Hagstrom, 1965:92-98). In contrast, where competition is weaker, pressure for quick processing will also be weaker

The Office of Science Information Service of the National Science Foundation has published information concerning the tempo of processing in journals in various fields; its data for three of the fields (National Science Foundation, 1964: 8) are reproduced in Table 2-12.

Table 2-12. Characteristics of Processing by Journals in
Mathematics, Chemistry and the Social Sciences

	Discipline		
	Mathematics	**Chemistry**	**Social Sciences**
1. Average processing time per paper	10 mos.	6.8 mos.	9.2 mos.
2. Average no. of papers per journal under review simultaneously	46	99	31
3. Average no. of papers in backlog simultaneously	29	121	32
4. Backlog as a percentage of no. of papers published per year	50%	29%	45%

The average processing time per published paper is shorter in chemistry than in mathematics or the social sciences, and this is true despite the fact that more papers are under review and in the backlog in journals in chemistry. The efficiency of processing, as measured by backlog as a percentage of the total number of pages published, is also greater in chemistry. More significant, however, is the fact that in the journals of mathematics processing times and levels of efficiency are more comparable to those in journals of the social sciences. Given that the level of normative integration is higher in mathematics than in the social sciences, these results suggests that in mathematics anomie is greater than in the social sciences. Insofar as the lengthy processing time of the social science periodicals is due to relatively greater dissensus, the data in Table 2-12 support the hypothetical ranking of disciplines shown in Figures 2-1 and 2-3.

Unfortunately, the N.S.F. reported aggregated, not separate data on the various social sciences. In addition, many of the most prestigious political science journals were omitted from the analysis. It is my impression, however, that these journals are much like those in the social sciences generally which *are* reported. The *American Political Science Review*, for example, in regularly published listings of its backlog of articles and the issues in which they are likely to appear shows intervals of about nine months, and if one assumes that its review procedure takes from four to six weeks (Ranney, 1969:168), one would estimate an average processing time of about ten months.

It has often been noted that the social sciences are the last stronghold of publication of scientific research in book form and consequently the findings presented in Table 2-12 are not strictly comparable since only journals are analyzed. Unfortunately, it is impossible to estimate how much the inclusion of books would alter the interval shown for political science, because of the lack of information about the proportion of work so published, and the length of time required for publication. It is almost certain that, if known, such information would yield a measure which would register relatively weak competition in political science. This is because publication of research in book form is usually possible only in fields where competition for priority is not prevalent.

To turn now to a further characteristic of scientific disciplines which should be responsive to their functional integration: Price's "immediacy factor"— the degree to which research papers in a given discipline cite recent rather than earlier papers—varies widely between fields (Price, 1970). Once again, however, it is not clear that the immediacy factor is uniquely determined by either normative or functional integration; instead it seems to be a function of both. Thus in a field characterized by little normative integration, one would expect authors to cite older "classic" papers and books in setting their work in a relevant theoretical context. On the other hand, in disciplines where knowledge of such a context can be assumed of the readers, cited matter may more often be drawn from the recent pertinent literature. Similarly, in a field characterized by little functional integration scientists may not know about recent work bearing on their research. In general then, one would expect fields highly integrated both normatively and functionally to exhibit higher immediacy factors than would be true of fields characterized by less of either type of integration. Data on the immediacy coefficients for selected journals in various disciplines have been presented by Price (1970:13-21), and his findings on the most recent issues of various journals are reproduced in Table 2-13.

Although there is variation within each of the three sets of journals, it appears that the relative rankings of the three fields in terms of their immediacy coefficients correspond to the relative rankings presented in Table 2-12. Chemistry journals tend to have the highest proportion of references to work published within the last five years, mathematics and the social science journals having somewhat lower proportions. Once again, one may argue that since mathematics is more highly integrated normatively than is political science, the former's relatively low immediacy coefficients are evidence of its relatively low functional integration.

In addition, the average number of references per article tends to be lowest in mathematics. Price suggested that this variable provides another measure of the social linkage in a discipline. Although one might object that it should be standardized for differences in length of article from field to field, it is unlikely that this factor can account for the difference between mathematics and the other disciplines reported in Table 2-13, since it has been shown that mathematical articles tend to be longer, in number of pages and number of words, than articles in chemistry or the social sciences (National Science Foundation, 1964:5-6). Of course, the fewer references per paper in mathematics may also be attributable to the fact that mathematics is a formal science; when standards of proof are clear, there is not as great a need to note the corroborative findings of others, a less likely condition in the empirical sciences. This explanation is not incompatible with the argument that the smaller number of references per paper in mathematics reflects its poorer functional

Table 2-13. Price's "Immediacy Coefficient" in Recent Issues of Selected Journals in Mathematics, Chemistry, and Various Social Sciences

	No. of Articles Examined	Average No. of References per Article	Immediacy Coefficient
Mathematics			
American Journal of Mathematics	12	9	29
American Mathematical Monthly	52	3	30
Journal of Mathematical Analysis and Application	27	8	37
Chemistry			
Journal of the American Chemical Society	52	17	50
Journal of Analytical Chemistry	60	9	45
Journal of Biological Chemistry	7	30	52
Journal of Inorganic Chemistry	50	16	54
Journal of Physical Chemistry	10	21	40
Social Sciences			
Journal of Politics	8	29	34
Public Opinion Quarterly*			38
American Sociological Review	8	25	35
Psychological Bulletin*			38
Journal of Educational Psychology*			52
American Educ. Research Journal*			36
Journal of Political Economy	14	14	52

*Price presents information for the entire period between 1960 and 1965 on this journal, but not information on the number of articles examined or the average number of references per paper.

integration. A high degree of consensus on standards of proof (one element of normative integration) may facilitate the reduction of functional integration insofar as it eliminates the need for corroboration.

In summary, although one would hesitate to attribute much support to the claim that mathematics is less integrated functionally than is either chemistry or political science on the basis of any one of these indirect measures of functional integration, in conjunction they afford it more substantial support.

Conclusion

The arguments advanced in this chapter imply that it is inappropriate to characterize variation among scientific disciplines in terms of a single dimension. Attempts to do so (Downey, 1969) have little utility in the search to understand the great variety of science's manifestations. For example, most prominent in discussions of differences among scientific fields is the "hard science-soft science" dimension, but there is little agreement about the nature of the categorization. It has been interpreted in terms of agreement on a theoretical and methodological perspective (Klaw, 1968:273-277), the practical import of a field's theories (Price, 1970:4), the extent to which a field's theories are formulated mathematically (Storer, 1967), or to which research is organized in contemporary "research fronts" rather than of archival literatures (Price, 1970:15-16)—and probably a host of other conceptions. It should be clear that the rankings of fields according to these various interpretations are not pefectly correlated, a circumstance demonstrated well in, for instance, mathematics and theoretical physics.

In short, the meaning of the "hard science-soft science" distinction is unclear and usually left implicit even in scholarly discussions. It would appear that more than one analytic dimension is involved in the distinction, and it has been shown above that most of the interpretations of the "hard science-soft science" dimension can be summarized in terms of normative and functional integration.

CHAPTER 3

ROUTINE IN SCIENTIFIC RESEARCH

Most discussions of scientific research simply identify it as a specific instance of the general category, professional work. Relative to most other types of work in industrial societies, professional work is characterized by the worker's formal freedom to choose the objects and techniques of his labor. Since other work often lacks this quality, scientific research, along with the work performed in other professions such as medicine and the law, is often depicted as an ideal form of labor, unmarred by the alienation from work which results from the absence of freedom. Unfortunately, treatment of scientific research as an ideal type (both in the normative and in the analytic sense) tends to obscure variations, for although research may be a relatively homogeneous activity in comparison to other forms of labor in industrial societies, it does exhibit systematic variation, especially across scientific disciplines.

Ironically, this differentiation is ignored in conceptions of the inherent variability of research. Discussions of scientific productivity and creativity tend to be phrased in terms of concepts such as "individual genius," to portray research as heavily dependent upon nonrational insight and personal inspiration, and to focus on the practices of individual scientists and the nature of scientific elites.[1] In societies where research is an occupation as well as a vocation, it is doubtful whether emphasis on individual differences can produce an adequate picture of the various patterns which characterize modern science.

---

[1]For a good example of this tendency, see Hadamard's critique of a survey of the research practices of mathematicians carried out through the periodical *L' Enseignment Mathematique* in the early 1900's (Hadamard, 1954: 10-11).

In this chapter I outline some differences, by discipline, in the typical work patterns of scientists. As in the previous chapter, my purpose is to show that a series of such differences may be interpreted in terms of a few general concepts, of which the most important summarizing concept is that of routinism. A short discussion of a previous use of this concept will clarify its meaning and illuminate some of its strengths and weaknesses when applied to the analysis of scientific work.

The Concept of Routine

Industrial sociologists have found that routinism is an important determinant of reactions to work. This is a factor emphasized by Blauner (1964) in his treatment of what determines how workers experience their work. He shows that industries based upon standardized machine and assembly-line techniques exhibit high degrees of routinism and high proportions of alienated workers, as compared to craft industries, on the one hand, and production by continuous process, on the other. Blauner's discussion shows the wide range of routinization among these types of industries.

> Craft technology and traditional manual skill create an unique-task rhythm in which there is involvement in the present situation on the basis of images of the future completion of the product or task.
>
> On the other hand, the unskilled routine jobs in the standardized machine and assembly line industries foster a repetitive-cycle work rhythm, a detachment from present tasks, and a concern with the future cessation of the activity itself, rather than the completion of specific tasks.
>
> Continuous-process technology and the work of monitoring automatic equipment results in still another rhythm, one that is new and unique in factory settings. It is the variety and unpredictability of the "calm-and-crisis" mode of time experience that is probably the most liberating. There are periods of routine activity when such tasks as instrument reading and patrolling are carried out, periods of waiting and relaxing when the routine work is done and operations are smooth, and also periods of intense activity when emergency breakdowns must be controlled (1964:174).

The central element in these comparisons is the extent to which work seems to have a uniform flow of its own. Blauner claims that when workers can control the direction and flow of their work, or when it is periodically subject to unpredictable emergencies, they are more committed and more absorbed by it.

On the other hand, Blauner's remarks elucidate one of the difficulties in applying the idea of routinism to variation in patterns of scientific work. It is clear that most varieties of scientific work are highly unroutinized compared to the kinds of industrial work which Blauner discusses. Even the most routine forms of scientific work (a commonly cited example here is the operation of high energy particle accelerators) are far less routine than work in craft or continuous-process industries. Thus in terms of routinism varieties of scientific work must involve very small differences at one pole of the continuum.

In addition, it is doubtful whether the concept of routinism pertains to a single feature of work. For example, a type of work may be characterized by a certain rate of disruptions or exceptions, on the one hand, and by the more or less effective attempts of workers to deal with interruptions, on the other. Perrow (1967) has shown that these two features of work are not perfectly correlated—some activities involve few exceptions but ineffective means of dealing with that few, and others, where there are many exceptions, have effective means to control them.[2] Thus the degree to which a given type of work may be described as routine is a function both of the number of discontinuities in the work itself and of the workers' ability to make effective adaptations to them. Discussion of the routinism of work should therefore distinguish between these two sources of order and progress.

In the following pages, I use the concept of routinism as the central element in characterizing patterns of research in mathematics, chemistry, and political science. My presentation is vulnerable to the difficulties mentioned above. If research in chemistry is said to be more routine than that in mathematics, it probably means there is a small absolute difference at the non-routine end of the continuum. However, the importance of such apparently small differences is an empirical question to be investigated in the remainder of this chapter. Similarly, I attempt to assess how much the two sources of routinism described above contribute to its overall levels in research in the three fields studied.

The concept of routinism does more than serve merely as a shorthand statement of the various impediments to everyday scientific work. On a broader scale, it has commonly been associated with concepts such as the division of labor, efficiency, and planning.

In addition, it may be expected that variations in routinism are associated with differential reactions to work as a personal experience. In general, the risk of frustration is a price of formal freedom. Scientists are formally free to do work that others judge to be creative, but creative work is almost by definition not routine. Lack of progress for varying periods afflicts almost all scientists in their research. On the other hand, insofar as they determine the scope and direction of their own work they must also muster the effort and command the ability to carry it through; consequently, frustration in research is considered to be prima-facie evidence of incompetence. When research workers are free to do as they wish, they tend to engage in whatever they choose, and if they fail in the chosen pursuit it is often interpreted as evidence of their inadequacy. Thus they are likely to become frustrated and depressed on encountering difficulties. Variation in the extent of routine in work in different fields should therefore be associated with difference in attitude toward the self as well as to work.

My aim, therefore, is not only to determine the relative extent of routine in research in the fields under study, but also to show its implications for other (correlated) facets of research. The discussion will supplement the previous chapter's consideration of differences in the social-organizational

---

[2]Thomas S. Kuhn (1961: 48) has suggested, independently of Perrow, that these two dimensions are important in signaling breakdowns of paradigms in science.

characteristics of disciplines; both topics are central to an understanding of scientific work.

Routinism in the Formal and Empirical Sciences

It is commonly noted that research in the formal sciences appears to be considerably less routinized than that in the empirical sciences. This difference can be illustrated by stereotypes of the settings in which scholars cry their "Eureka's!" It is difficult, for example, to imagine a chemist making an important discovery in any setting other than a laboratory filled with bubbling flasks and tubes. In contrast, no corresponding stereotype exists in mathematics, and the closest thing to one, Poincare's trolley-car step, is only a single incident.

Arguments based upon stereotypes are always suspect, but an argument may be constructed linking typical settings in which work is carried out and the relative extent of routine found there. A typical setting for research usually implies typical associated techniques. The conception of technique here used is a broad one that includes all actions which individuals perform upon objects (including symbols) in order to make some change in them (Perrow, 1967:195). When the worker can rely upon a certain program of action to carry him to his goal, his work is defined as routine, in contrast to work for which he has no such program of action. Thus a typical setting for research is positively associated with a relative amount of routine.

Research in the formal sciences appears to be based upon less efficacious techniques than that in the empirical sciences. This is probably a consequence of the fact that the former's theories are distinguished by not being subject to empirical proof. Whereas in the empirical sciences much of the work involves the collection and analysis of empirical information, this is usually not the case in the formal sciences. Although the prerequisite of empirical evidence does not automatically imply an effective method of collecting and analyzing data, one may expect in the established empirical sciences some degree of efficacy in technique. Consequently, one would also expect more routine work in the empirical sciences than in the formal sciences.

A partial test of some of these hypotheses is afforded by responses to a question I asked scientists in the three fields. In order to include a wide variety of data- and evidence-gathering activities, and also to encourage variation in the responses of mathematicians, I asked respondents to report how often, in general, they experience difficulty in obtaining information or data relevant to research. Their responses are shown in Table 3-1.

Although the question was phrased in a very general manner, 20 percent of the mathematicians reported that their research did not involve gathering data or information, in contrast to the chemists and political scientists, none of whom said that was their situation. The political scientists reported more difficulty than did the chemists, confirming the hypothesis that data-gathering is less a routine matter among the former.

From this evidence it might appear that research in mathematics is *more* routine than it is in the empirical sciences, since mathematicians are not as subject to interruptions made necessary by data-collecting as are empiri-

Table 3-1. Frequency of Difficulty in Obtaining Information or Data, by Discipline

Frequency of Difficulty	Discipline		
	Mathematics	Chemistry	Political Science
Almost always	4%	5%	11%
Often	18	25	36
Sometimes	41	55	47
Never	17	15	7
Question not applicable to work	20	0	0
	100%	100%	100%
N	(179)	(217)	(210)

cal scientists. I argue, however that empirical scientists may routinize their data-collecting and make it predictable, and this advantage is denied the mathematicians. Let us begin by examining the mathematicians' perceptions of predictability.

Mathematicians most often describe their work in terms of such non-routine elements as chance, irrationality, and the unconscious (Hadamard, 1954). In recounting their experiences, those I interviewed in the early stages of this study made statements of which the following are examples:

> When you're working on a problem you spend a lot of time just digging to try to understand it. Then sometimes the understanding will come in as little time as a microsecond. Once you understand the problem, the solution can come very quickly, but it's often not easy to obtain the understanding.

> It's pretty hard to get anywhere in this field with just hard work. I'm usually working in a general area rather than on a specific question. Once in a while I'll have an insight about what is going on and, as a result, I'll be able to write down a theorem.

> I waste a lot of time doing the same thing over and over and apparently getting nowhere. Sometimes I spend literally weeks to find a two-line proof. Usually, I'm just waiting around for something to happen.

I found the mathematicians reluctant to describe their research in terms of typical stages or patterns. Of course, research in any field is not a routine pursuit and scientists usually avoid constructing formal descriptions of it, except perhaps when they write textbooks. But even given this degree of resistance as a baseline, mathematicians were relatively unwilling to identify any stages or activities as being routine or automatic portions of their research. This gave me good reason to believe that routine may be much more prevalent in the empirical than in the formal sciences.

The Progress and Planning of Scientific Research

Routine is work with its own uniform rate of progress. The archetype is the assembly line, with its constant speed, and its consequently constant rate of productivity. On the other hand, unroutinized work, such as scientific research, is characterized by wide variation in rates of progress. Progress in research, as in other creative endeavors, is precarious and sudden halt is as unpredictable as sudden inspiration. Once again, however, there is reason to believe there is systematic variation in this between disciplines. If mathematicians, in comparison to empirical scientists, lack routine means of producing research results, then there should be large proportions of their time when apparently they make no progress. In fact, during my early interviews, mathematicians frequently admitted it:

> I feel that I'm stuck most of the time. The real question seems to be whether or not there is any period when I'm not stuck.

> Some of my problems just don't seem to be solvable. You can attack them for so long, you can talk to others about them, but you still don't make any progress. Then after a while you just give up.

I questioned my respondents about the frequency of periods of little or no progress in their research, and found that mathematicians' responses (Table 3-2) are consistent with the hypothesis that progress in their research frequently comes to a standstill—a complaint less common among chemists and political scientists.[3]

As pointed out earlier, however, the incidence of lack of progress in research is a function of both the flow of the work itself and of adaptation to the conditions which may thwart endeavor. The extent to which research workers in a given discipline successfully employ adaptive techniques to reduce disruption may serve as a measure of routine as a product of those techniques, as opposed to the flow of work itself. For example: if political scientists employ adaptive techniques to a much greater extent than do chemists, it might be concluded that although the research of the former is less routine they are able to overcome the lack and achieve as much freedom from lack of progress as chemists enjoy.

But what kinds of adaptive techniques can research workers employ to ward off impediments to research? Just as individuals in highly routine work often seek to introduce into it non-routine and disruptive features (Walker and Guest, 1952: Ch. 10, 13), so, too, those in highly unroutinized work often seek to introduce routine features. One means to routinize research is to exert personal control over it through conscious planning. By setting up time schedules, deadlines, and special periods devoted entirely to given

---

[3]The wording of the question on which Table 3-3 is based would appear to allow the possibility that older scholars in each field would report more difficulty than younger scholars because older scholars have had more exposure to the risk of it than have younger ones. if this were true, then it would be inappropriate to interpret the results in this table as indications of the *rates* in each field. In fact, however, there is no correlation between years of experience and reported extent of these difficulties in any of the fields. The correlations for mathematics, chemistry, and political science are, respectively, .07, −.01, and .01.

Table 3-2. **Frequency of Encountering Barriers to Progress in Research, by Discipline**

Frequency of Encountering Barriers to Progress	Discipline		
	Mathematics	Chemistry	Political Science
This has been a common experience in my research.	59%	21%	26%
I have experienced difficulties several times, but they are not common.	32	52	45
I have experienced such difficulties only rarely	6	25	27
I have never experienced such difficulties.	2	2	2
	99%	100%	100%
N	(182)	(218)	(210)

tasks, scientists try to bring certainty into what may otherwise seem to be highly uncertain activity. There are obvious limits to the efficacy of these strategies. In the case of tasks where there seems to be no relationship between time expenditures and output, the conscious planning of work will have little, if any, effect on productivity. Thus in fields like mathematics where productivity seems to depend more upon insight than upon the amount of time spent thinking about problems,[4] scientists see no benefit in extensive planning. On the other hand, on tasks that have been routinized to a high degree, they need not try to increase the element of certainty. The assembly line is perhaps the limiting case: where work imposes its own flow and pace upon the worker, planning on his part is superfluous. Thus to the extent that there is more routine in research in chemistry than in political science, one would expect less planning in the former than in the latter.

These arguments assume that planning is only a response to the non-routine nature of a particular task, but this is clearly an unwarranted assumption. For example, although assembly-line work is routine, if the worker is responsible for initiating and maintaining the operation of the assembly line, he must plan in order to insure the presence of the necessary equipment and materials. Given the technical demands of their experimental procedures, chemists are probably more liable to need to plan everyday research activities than either

---

[4]These are not necessarily independent. Several of the mathematicians whom I interviewed asserted that the greater the experience in the field, the more likely are such insights, (contradicting the popular notion that productivity and creativity in mathematics are associated with youth). In the *short run,* however, time spent working on a problem and the ability to have new insights about it seem to be unrelated.

mathematicians or political scientists. Thus, in order to demonstrate that political scientists attempt to introduce routine into their research by engaging in planning, it is necessary to show that this planning is not the result of the technical requirements of their research procedures.

I asked my respondents to indicate to what extent they set deadlines, such as commitments to give public lectures, to force themselves to complete research by a certain date. This form of planning should not be highly dependent upon the daily requirements of operating and maintaining a research apparatus. Following the hypothesis that political scientists attempt to routinize their research to a greater extent than mathematicians or chemists, responses to the question should show that political scientists practice this form of planning to a greater extent than scholars in the other two fields. The replies in Table 3-3 are consistent with the argument. Mathematicians, who probably

Table 3-3. **Frequency of Using Deadlines to Force the Completion of Work, by Discipline**

| Frequency of Using Deadlines | | Discipline | |
	Mathematics	Chemistry	Political Science
Rarely, if ever	56%	42%	15%
Sometimes	35	42	50
Often	7	12	27
Almost always	1	4	8
	99%	100%	100%
N	(181)	(217)	(211)

Table 3-4. **Frequency of Planning a Day's Work, by Discipline**

| Frequency of Planning a Day's Work | | Discipline | |
	Mathematics	Chemistry	Political Science
Rarely, if ever	47%	29%	22%
Sometimes	36	38	40
Often	15	27	30
Almost always	2	6	8
	100%	100%	100%
N	(182)	(214)	(209)

derive little benefit from scheduling work, are least in the habit; chemists, whose work is probably more routine than mathematicians' or political scientists' because of their greater use of standardized experimental procedures, show an intermediate pattern.

I also asked my respondents to report the extent to which they plan a day's work in detail. Since this kind of planning should be more highly dependent on the requirements of operating and maintaining an experimental apparatus, the above arguments lead one to expect that responses to the question will show a higher relative utilization of this kind of planning by chemists. Table 3-4 presents the responses to the question, and they meet the expectation. Once again, mathematicians do the smallest amount of planning, but now the differences between chemists and political scientists are quite small. Thus the results are consistent with the hypothesis that whereas daily planning is used by political scientists for the routinization of a nonroutine task, it is required of chemists primarily because of their techniques.[5]

I have argued that research cannot be as thoroughly routinized in mathematics as in the empirical sciences; that this is reflected by the lower rates of planning shown in Tables 3-3 and 3-4; and that while work in political science is less routine than it is in chemistry, still it may be routinized to such an extent that discontinuities in research among political scientists may be almost as infrequent as among chemists. Supporting these arguments are the responses to a question I asked about the perception of efficiency in one's work. (Table 3-5).

As expected, mathematicians perceive lower efficiency than do chemists and political scientists, while the perception of the last-named resembles that of chemists. These findings are consistent with the argument that political scientists must plan their work more thoroughly than do chemists if they are to reach the latter's high degree of perceived efficiency. Mathematicians, however, see themselves as inefficient workers and their lower rates of planning suggest that they do not resort to the conscious planning of work as a corrective.

Thus far, all the evidence presented in support of the above arguments has been in the form of scientists' *perceptions* of their work. One might therefore question whether these reflect anything more than differences in the stereotypes of work between fields. Responses to a question about the perceived efficiency of work would seem to be particularly open to this criticism since they are not based on clear and objective standards of judgment. On the other hand, the concept of efficiency is clearly related to the objective

---

[5]Indirect evidence supporting this hypothesis might be provided by intradisciplinary correlations between the extent to which a scientist plans daily work in detail and the extent to which he encounters barriers to progress. If daily planning is not as necessary for the avoidance of difficulty in chemistry as in political science, the latter field should show a higher negative correlation than does the former. Although this is the case, both correlations are quite small: in chemistry it is $-.09$ and in political science it is $-.15$. The smallness of this difference and the small differences in the distribution of responses to the question about daily planning may also be partially due to the fact that the question does not refer specifically to a scientist's research. However, this was at least the implicit reference of the entire questionnaire.

Table 3-5.   Frequency of Working Highly Efficiently, by Discipline

Frequency of Working Highly Efficiently	Discipline		
	Mathematics	Chemistry	Political Science
Rarely, if ever	11%	5%	3%
Sometimes	60	54	49
Often	27	34	42
Almost Always	2	7	6
	100%	100%	100%
N	(180)	(211)	(209)

results of work since it is formally defined as the ratio of output over time spent. It is therefore a question whether perceptions of efficiency, which may be called subjective efficiency, are related to work output, objective efficiency.

Unfortunately, it is impossible to construct correlations between objective and subjective efficiency in each of the three fields because I have no information about actual time spent on research. However, the study did contain questions which allow the computation of the amount of time scientists estimate that they spend on research in a typical week. Hence it is possible to examine the relationships of subjective efficiency and the ratio of scientists' estimates of the time spent on research to their output, as measured by number of publications.

The formal definition of efficiency implies the formula Output = Time × Efficiency. When dealing with estimates of time and efficiency, however, it is probably more parsimonious to use as a model Output = Estimated Time + Subjective Efficiency.[6] By restating the relationships in terms of a linear model and employing multiple regression analysis to estimate its parameters, one can further test some of these hypotheses. Two hypotheses may give a demonstration: First, given a highly standardized work procedure, there should be little independent association between output and subjective perception of efficiency. In such situations output should be primarily a function of time, and the standardized regression coefficient of the amount of time spent on work should be larger than the standardized regression coefficient of subjective efficiency. Since chemistry is alleged to have the most highly standardized procedures of the three fields, one can determine if this

---

[6]In addition to this model, I have examined models which postulate various kinds of interaction effects of the two independent variables. Since none of these account for more variance in the dependent variable than the simple linear model, and since they yield similar substantive conclusions, I will not present them here. The measure of publication productivity used in the following analysis if the natural logarithm of a scientist's total number of publications in 1968 (plus 1.0, so that all raw scores are non-zero).

pattern is displayed by chemistry's standardized regression coefficients. Second, one would expect certain differences in the sizes of unstandardized regression coefficients by discipline. For example, unstandardized regression coefficients of time spent on research should be larger where work is relatively routine than where it is less so. Similarly, where research can be accomplished by a variety of strategies and procedures, each being effective in the production of results, unstandardized regression coefficients of subjective efficiency should reflect higher independent associations with objective productivity than where there are no known effective techniques or where research is highly routine and therefore almost exclusively a function of time.

Data relevant to these last hypotheses are shown in Table 3-6, where the unstandardized regression coefficients of the regression of number of publications on subjective efficiency and estimated time spent on research are presented. The results presented are consistent with the arguments above about the nature of research in the three fields. The claim that research in chemistry is more routine than it is in mathematics or political science is supported by chemistry's relatively large regression coefficient for estimated time spent on research. Similarly, the claim that productivity is more a matter of ameliorative action in political science than it is in mathematics (where such action is not available) or in chemistry (where productivity is more a function of time) is supported by the relatively large regression coefficient for subjective efficiency found in political science. The data presented in Table 3-6 do not bear on the question of the relative size of the independent associations of estimated time and subjective efficiency with research in chemistry, since the answer would require the presentation of the standardized

Table 3-6. **Regression of Number of Publications on Estimated Time Spent on Research and Subjective Efficiency, by Discipline**

	Discipline					
	Mathematics		**Chemistry**		**Political Science**	
Statistics	*b*	*t*	*b*	*t*	*b*	*t*
Regression coefficients and t-values of estimated time spent on research work	.004	.472	.025	4.776	.003	1.007
Regression coefficients and t-values of estimated efficiency	.031	1.114	.100	1.302	.139	3.207
Coefficients of determination (R^2)	.01		.12		.06	
F-values of coefficients of determination	.823		13.351		6.226	
N	(166)		(206)		(196)	

regression coefficients of each variable. The t-values shown for chemistry clearly hint at the result of the standardization of the regression coefficients, however, and the standardized coefficient of estimated time is .32, in contrast to a value of .09 for the standardized coefficient of subjective efficiency.

This section, then, presents evidence which both supports the arguments made above and traces some of the implications of variation in the routinism in research. In empirical sciences where research is aided by well-established and effective techniques, it tends to be more standardized and routine than elsewhere. In fields like chemistry, work has a rhythm of its own, so that concern with efficiency and attempts to improve it are less prominent than in fields like political science. On the other hand, research in the formal sciences tends to be less routine and at the same time lends itself less to routinization than is the case in the empirical sciences. Like political scientists, mathematicians engage in work which does not have its own rhythm and routine; unlike political scientists, however, they are unable effectively to employ simple strategies for imposing their own order on their work. Since research is not as amenable to efficiency-improving strategies in mathematics as it is in political science, efficiency is not as salient in the former, and subjective perception of efficiency is not as highly correlated with productivity. Thus in the formal sciences, research is seen as primarily dependent upon personal inspiration and insight, and neither of these factors have their own rhythm, nor are they amenable to conscious planning.

The Division of Labor in Scientific Research

There is a strong tendency toward division of labor in routine. When an activity can be divided among competent specialists who apply their expertise to limited sub-tasks, efficiency is increased, and this is as true of scientific research as of other work. Of course, the bureaucratization and standardization of scientific research may entail dysfunctional consequences at the same time as increased efficiency, consequences which have been widely discussed by sociologists of science (Hagstrom, 1965:152-154). The important point, however, is that to the extent that the process consists of routine tasks, one can expect scientists to organize their work among groups rather than to maintain individualistic patterns of work organization. As is the case of other forms of work, division of labor in scientific research often enhances the scientist's competitive position (Hagstrom, 1965:111-112).

Among American academic scientists, the most usual form of division of labor is that between professor-directed graduate students, post-doctorate fellows, and technicians.[7] Differences between disciplines in the prevalence of this form are well known, and Table 3-7 presents information about the numbers of subordinates directed in this way by my respondents.

In the light of the hypotheses presented above about the relative degree of

---

[7]This organizational form involves a division of labor, but it cannot be described as a bureaucracy. The latter form involves greater specialization, formalization, and hierarchy of authority than is typical of professor-directed teams of scientific workers. Routine work appears to foster this traditional structure in academic science, at least, rather than in large bureaucratic organizations.

Table 3-7. **Means and Standard Deviations of Number of Subordinates per Respondent, by Discipline**

	Discipline					
	Mathematics		Chemistry		Political Science	
Type of Subordinate	$\overline{X}$	S.D.	$\overline{X}$	S.D.	$\overline{X}$	S.D.
Graduate Student	2.16	2.56	4.13	3.44	4.71	4.96
Postdoctoral Fellow	.21	.66	.74	1.42	.10	.44
Technician	.20	.99	.61	1.38	.60	1.48
N	(182)		(217)		(212)	

routine in research, one might expect to find the largest number of subordinates in chemistry and fewer in mathematics and political science. If mathematicians face inherently nonroutine tasks, and if political scientists must expend a great deal of effort to routinize their work, presumably a large number of subordinates would impede them; and, indeed, the large number of subordinates under the direction of political scientists is somewhat surprising. On the other hand, the hypothesis that scientists will divide the labor of routine tasks implies that routine is a sufficient, but not a necessary condition of attempts to divide that labor. It is therefore possible that scientists might supervise large numbers of students and technicians who, nevertheless, contribute little to the scientists' research.

Since numbers alone do not necessarily establish the value of subordinates to research, information is needed on their contribution in order to test adequately my earlier argument. One form of information consists of scientists' perception of the extent of their use of subordinates, and I therefore questioned my respondents on the point.

In Table 3-8 it is shown that subordinates are involved in the chemists' research to a much greater extent than is true of either mathematicians or political scientists. Thus, even though political scientists supervise as many graduate students and research technicians as do chemists, their subordinates' contribution to their research is perceived as smaller.

The adequacy of these perceptions may be checked by examining the correlations in each field between the number of subordinates a scientist directs and his productivity—a check which is not definitive because the output of research may be reciprocally related to the number of subordinates supervised. Nevertheless, if such correlations are very small in size, it is reasonable to conclude that subordinates contribute little to research.

The findings reported in Table 3-9 generally reflect the judgments presented in Table 3-8, although the correlations in political science are much closer to those in mathematics than the distribution of responses in the same two fields presented in Table 3-8. Except for the correlations between output

Table 3-8.   Perceived Involvement of Subordinates, by Discipline

	Discipline		
Response	**Mathematics**	**Chemistry**	**Political Science**
All of my research involves their work	1%	28%	4%
Most of my research involves their work	11	65	24
They sometimes play a role in my research but I do most of my research alone	48	6	61
My research is independent of them	41	1	11
	101%	100%	100%
N	(182)	(217)	(213)

Table 3-9.   Correlations Between Number of Subordinates and Supervisors' Productivity, by Discipline

	Discipline					
	Mathematics		**Chemistry**		**Political Science**	
Type of Subordinate	r	N	r	N	r	N
Graduate Student	.04	(181)	.51	(217)	.03	(212)
Postdoctoral Fellow	.04	(183)	.52	(217)	.18	(213)
Technician	.03	(183)	−.03	(217)	−.03	(212)

and number of technicians, large numbers of subordinates are strongly associated with high rates of productivity in chemistry, but not in mathematics or political science.

Graduate students who contribute to the research of their professors may come to believe that they are being exploited, being especially likely to do so because, like their professors, they value independence (Hagstrom, 1965: 105-111). Such an attitude may serve as an additional indicator of the magnitude of the graduate students' contribution to research. Hagstrom reports that among a sample of recent recipients of the doctorate in chemistry, 49%

reported that "major professors often exploit doctoral candidates." The corresponding figures from similar samples from political science and mathematics were 30% and 28% respectively (Hagstrom, 1965:134).

Finally, an overall index of the importance of others in a scientist's research is provided by the proportion of his papers that are co-authored. This index is more general than the measures discussed above because it includes contributions from professional peers as well as from students and technicians. One would expect the analysis of co-authorship to yield the same general pattern as the variables discussed above: to the extent that research is routine, scientists coordinate their work with others. And, as it proves, only among chemists are there very high proportions of co-authored papers (Table 3-10).

There is, then, a good deal of evidence that subordinates and peers make greater contributions to a given scientist's research if he is in chemistry than in mathematics or political science, and therefore that research in chemistry is more routine. Even though political science and chemistry are both empirical, research in the former is not as routine as it is in the latter, where the division of labor is more prevalent and more efficacious.

Following Hagstrom it may be argued that a division of labor is to be found in scientific research only when there is competition (1965:222-226). It might be, then, that since competition for recognition is less intense in political science than in chemistry (as has been shown), the relative absence of division of labor in political science is not due to a hypothetical lack of routine in research.

There are several reasons for rejecting this argument in the present case. First, as already noted, political scientists expend at least as much effort as chemists in planning their research, and evidence presented below shows that political scientists become more upset about difficulties in their research than chemists do. These conditions seem to contradict the notion that political scientists are not motivated to increase the efficiency and productivity of their work because there is so little competition for priority in their discipline. Second, attributing the division of labor to competition cannot account for the difference in the correlations between number of subordinates and output in chemistry and political science. Since the mean number of subordinates in each field is roughly the same, and since there is substantial variation within each field in the number which the individual scientist supervises, the low correlations in political science (Table 3-9) cannot be due either to failure to recruit help or to lack of variation in number of subordinates. On the other hand, the differences in the size of this correlation are directly implied by the hypothesis that research is more routine in chemistry than it is in political science.

These comments do not imply that accounting for the division of labor in scientific research in terms of competition is necessarily inconsistent with the hypothesis concerning routine. In the long run, at least, competition for recognition may lead scientists to prefer forms of research which permit routine,[8] and routine may, in turn, lead to keener competition. Competition

---

[8]This hypothesis is similar to one suggested by Collins concerning the relation between competition for recognition in a field and the development of it of empirical

and routine may therefore be joint determinants of the dividing of labor. In the case of political science, however, it appears that lack of routine rather than weak competition is responsible for the relative rarity of the division of labor.

Segregation of Work

Routine work tends to be a self-contained activity; its reciprocal relations with other spheres of life are few and weak when compared with those of other types of work. In modern mass-production industry, industrial workers engaged in routine often grow alienated and turn to other activities for the experiences and rewards once found in work (Dubin, 1956; Blauner, 1964: 15-34). When this is the case, work becomes purely instrumental; it is not a source of valued social experience.

The idea that routine tends to be more segregated from other activities than unroutinized work can be used to elaborate my hypotheses about the relative routine in the three fields. By examining the interdependence between research and other activities, one can both test and demonstrate some implications of the hypotheses.

Of course, most scientific work is unroutinized, in comparison with work on industrial assembly lines, and the dissociation of work from other activities experienced by industrial workers is not likely to prevail among scientists. To scientists, the important question is not whether work is a central life interest, but to what extent other activities affect it as a central life interest. Other interests, for example, may become exclusive preoccupations; scientists often complain that other concerns and obligations lay claim to time

Table 3-10.   Proportion of Scientists' Publications in 1966-69 Co-authored, by Discipline

Proportion of Papers Co-authored	Discipline		
	Mathematics	Chemistry	Political Science
None	40%	3%	41%
Less than ¼	20	1	23
¼ to ½	16	4	13
½ to ¾	13	9	13
More than ¾, but not all	5	31	6
All	5	52	4
	99%	100%	100%
N	(183)	(216)	(212)

methods and logical rigor. Collins argues that competition can foster the development of these features because they provide better conditions for waging and judging the results of competition than speculative methods do. (Collins, 1968: 133-135).

and effort they wish to reserve for their research. One would expect such situations to be least prevalent in the most routine types of scientific work. Work which has its own uniform flow is not as likely to be disrupted as it would be were its pace and direction dependent upon the worker. I asked my respondents to indicate to what extent their less productive periods result from the distraction of outside activities.

These response patterns (Table 3-11) are consistent with my earlier claim that, compared to mathematics and political science, research in chemistry has a flow of its own and chemists are, therefore, less likely to be distracted than are mathematicians and political scientists. Further support for this hypothesis is found in responses to a similar question on the extent to which personal problems in scientists' relationships reduce their productivity in research. Once again (Table 3-12) among chemists other interests and commitments appear to interfere with research work less than is the case among mathematicians and political scientists.

Table 3-11. **Frequency of Reports that Outside Distractions Cause Low Productivity, by Discipline**

		Discipline		
Frequency		**Mathematics**	**Chemistry**	**Political Science**
Never		27%	40%	24%
Sometimes		55	46	54
Often		18	13	22
		100%	99%	100%
	N	(180)	(216)	(209)

Table 3-12. **Frequency of Reports That Personal Problems Cause Low Productivity, by Discipline**

		Discipline		
Frequency		**Mathematics**	**Chemistry**	**Political Science**
Never		35%	53%	37%
Sometimes		53	38	51
Often		12	8	12
		100%	99%	100%
	N	(179)	(216)	(209)

At this point one might object that the results shown in Tables 3-11 and 3-12 do not provide evidence on the differential flow of research work in the three disciplines. Instead, the results might be attributed not to the flow of work itself, but to the fact that work in chemistry is carried out in a workplace, the laboratory, which is separated from the home, while this is not so true of mathematics and political science. Of course, the extent to which the workplace and the home are separated may not be independent of the routine of research; there is probably a positive association between the two variables. The question at issue, however, is whether the results in Tables 3-11 and 3-12 provide information on the routine of work, independent of the association between routine and the separation of home and workplace.

Chemists work at home less often than do mathematicians and political scientists (Table 3-13), and one cannot reject the alternative argument presented above on the ground that it is mistaken in its premise about the relative

Table 3-13.   Frequency of Working at Home, by Discipline

| | Discipline | | |
Frequency	Mathematics	Chemistry	Political Science
Rarely, if ever	5%	13%	10%
Sometimes	23	29	26
Often	44	44	35
Almost always	27	13	29
	99%	99%	100%
N	(182)	(217)	(212)

separation of home and workplace in the three fields. On the other hand, if there is a general positive relation between working at home and being interrupted at work, one would expect to observe this relationship within scientific fields as well as between them. I therefore calculated the correlations between frequency of working at home and the complaints presented in Tables 3-11 and 3-12 (Table 3-14).

Within the three disciplines it is not the case that men who frequently work at home are also aware of the most interference with their work: five of the six correlations in the table show a negative sign rather than the expected positive sign. Thus in view of the fact that there is a fair amount of variation in the frequency of working at home within each of the fields, it is doubtful whether any simple relation between the separation of home from workplace and the disruption of work by other concerns and interests can entirely account for the association between routine and segregation of work.

Alienation and Accountability

Thus far this examination of routine in scientific research has focused

Table 3-14.   Correlations Between Working at Home and Two Indicators of Interruption, by Discipline

Correlations Between Working at Home and:	Discipline					
	Mathematics		Chemistry		Political Science	
	r	N	r	N	r	N
1. Distraction by Outside Activities	−.06	(180)	.01	(215)	−.05	(211)
2. Distraction by Personal Problems	−.12	(179)	−.17	(215)	−.05	(208)

upon scientists' perceptions and upon various characteristics of the organization and performance of their work. We turn now to the matter of scientists' personal reactions. Previous studies of workers' reactions have revealed a positive correlation between routine and alienation from work (Blauner, 1964: 173-175). In its most extreme forms, alienation from work follows upon a radical dissociation of worker from work; he feels antipathy to it.

> In what does this alienation of labor consist? First that the work is *external* to the worker, that it is not a part of his nature, that consequently he does not fulfill himself in his work but denies himself, has a feeling of misery, not of well-being, does not develop freely a physical and mental energy, but is physically exhausted and mentally debased. The worker therefore feels himself at home only during his leisure, whereas at work he feels homeless. His work is not voluntary, but imposed, *forced labor*. It is not the satisfaction of a need, but only a means for satisfying other needs. Its alien character is clearly shown by the fact that as soon as there is no physical or other compulsion it is avoided like the plague. Finally, the alienated character of work for the worker appears in the fact that it is not his work but work for someone else, that in work he does not belong to himself but to another person. (Marx, 1964:169-170).

The personal and social pathologies associated with alienation from work are rarely found among academic scientists. Free to determine the direction and pace of their research, it is there they find self-expression. This does not mean, however, that research is without pathologies of its own. In contrast to most forms of routine, wherein limited autonomy is a major source of social and psychological disorders, the pathologies of unroutinized work, such as scientific research, are usually attributed to the workers' freedom and the consequent lack of regulation (Zetterberg, 1967). In the limiting case where the worker is completely free, being also simultaneously completely responsible for his work and without guidelines, he may become paralyzed by freedom, and some alienation or detachment from work may actually stimulate him.

Most men can explain what they do by appeal to the requirements of the job, or to the orders of the boss, or to the custom of the manor. But perfectly free choices reflect what kind of men we are. A man who designs cigarette-lighter mechanisms may never call his work "creative engineering," but because his job is specified and circumscribed, he need never ask himself whether he is, in fact, a creative person. In contrast, if my research project is not creative scholarship, it's because I'm not creative. For the scholar, each choice of a research topic or strategy is a choice of what kind of man to be.

Momentary depressions get magnified by this process. The passing doubt that new cigarette-lighter mechanisms are worth all the effort passes as the man with the designing job goes back to it. But passing doubt that a line of scholarly work is worthwhile stops the work, which keeps the work stopped (Stinchcombe, 1966:25-16).

Given the freedom associated with academic research, personality differences among scientists may be more important for successful role performance than they are in other groups. Merton, for example, states that the ability to avoid or ignore work-related frustration is an important difference between eminent scientists and their less distinguished colleagues.

Men of high eminence are generally men of exceptional ego-strength, with a marked sense of self-confidence (at the extreme, attractive arrogance). They tolerate frustration, absorbing repeated failure without manifest damage (1967; also 1968:60-62).

Merton also suggests that scientists who are able to tolerate failure without becoming frustrated or depressed are more likely to make significant discoveries than their colleagues who are equally talented but more easily discouraged. One might ask, however, if factors other than personality characteristics may account for differences in the response of individual scientists to failure to make progress in their research. In particular, one might expect that insofar as routine is positively associated with alienation or detachment, detachment may confer immunity from the disillusionment which can result from difficulties at work. If this is true, scientists in fields where work is relatively routine should show less frustration and depression than their colleagues in other disciplines. Since research is more routine in chemistry than in mathematics and political science, this argument leads to the prediction that chemists are less prone to frustration or depression than are mathematicians and political scientists.

Data consistent with this prediction are presented in Table 3-15. Although differences between the three fields' patterns of responses are not large, they do register a negative relationship between routine and the frequency of frustration or depression. The differences by discipline, shown in Table 3-15, may have been attenuated by the operation of other variables in addition to routine. For example, getting upset over difficulties in research is almost certainly a function of the scientist's competitive situation. This is probably true of other endeavors: a football placekicker is most likely to become upset about his failure to convert the point after a touchdown when his team is in a close contest. Similarly, a scientist may be expected to show more frustration when in a field that is highly competitive. Since competition is fiercer in chemistry than in either mathematics or political science (Chapter 2), it may be that

Table 3-15. **Frequency of Reports that Depression or Frustration Accompany Periods of Low Productivity, by Discipline**

	Discipline		
Frequency	Mathematics	Chemistry	Political Science
Never	7%	7%	8%
Only rarely	19	29	23
Sometimes	54	50	46
Almost always	19	14	24
	99%	100%	101%
N	(180)	(217)	(213)

chemists would suffer from less frustration than is apparent in Table 3-15 if their situation were as competitive as it is in mathematics and political science.

An alternative method of assessing chemists' relative alienation from research is inquiring into how they attribute responsibility for disruptions. Alienation or detachment from scientific research not only implies insulation from the frustration and depression which may result from lack of progress; it also implies that scientists will not feel personally responsible for it. When workers are alienated they attribute their output, or the lack of it, to factors other than their own ability or effort, but those who are not alienated attribute their output to themselves. Thus it should be possible to use scientists' perception that they themselves are responsible for their difficulties and failures as an indicator of the absence of alienation. In addition, perceptions of personal responsibility for difficulties in research are probably less dependent upon competition than is frustration. One might therefore expect the former to reflect detachment from research more faithfully than the latter.

I questioned my respondents on the extent to which their research difficulties are a consequence of personal inability; the distribution of responses for the three fields under study are presented in Table 3-16. As expected, the differences in mathematicians' and chemists' responses to this question are much larger than those shown in Table 3-15. On the other hand, the findings on the political scientists are inconsistent with the assumption that their pattern is similar to that of the mathematicians. Indeed, political scientists are as unlikely to blame their difficulties on their own lack of ability as are chemists. One might speculate that the scientists' perception of their failure to do their research may depend upon both alienation from work and the standards for making judgments about ability. In fields like political science where there is less consensus on standards of success and where average publishing rates are lower, differences in the scientists' ability may be related less to

Table 3-16. Frequency of Reports that Less Productive Periods Result From Lack of Ability, by Discipline

Frequency		Mathematics	Chemistry	Political Science
			Discipline	
Never		19%	31%	45%
Sometimes		59	63	51
Often		22	6	4
		100%	100%	100%
	N	(175)	(212)	(204)

their productivity and less apparent to them.[9] Thus the relatively little normative integration in their discipline may help political scientists to ward off doubts about their personal adequacy, regardless of their relative detachment from work.

In discussions of responsibility for success or failure there are commonly statements about personal effort as well as about ability, ability and effort being complementary and necessarily involved to some extent if a task is to be successful. But though these two features are theoretically independent, explanations of personal failure often show them as interdependent. Explaining failure by the absence of motivation is a less painful alternative than blaming oneself for lacking ability. As a result, bystanders often interpret a professed lack of motivation as the rationalization of actual inability. Moreover, the attributing of failure to lack of motivation and effort may in part reflect the attention and involvement required by the work itself. Thus one would expect the attribution to be negatively related to routinism in research: first, because nonroutine work does not allow as much personal detachment and, second, because it is therefore more likely to foster the rationalization of failure caused by personal inability. As a consequence, evidence concerning attribution of failure to lack of motivation and effort may be used to test the general hypothesis that research is more routine in chemistry than in mathematics and political science; but it does not reveal the particular sources of the attribution.

Mathematicians and political scientists have been shown to believe they are distracted by other responsibilities and activities to a greater extent than do chemists. Similar results ensued when I asked my respondents how much trouble they have in settling down to work (Table 3-17). Once again, among the three sets of scholars, mathematicians and political scientists report

---

[9]This condition may also be manifested in the often-noted lack of child prodigies in the social sciences. Compared to fields like mathematics and chemistry, the social sciences lack consensus on the standards by which excellence can be detected early.

Table 3-17. **Frequency of Reports of Trouble in Settling Down to Work, by Discipline**

| | Discipline | | |
Frequency	Mathematics	Chemistry	Political Science
Rarely, if ever	12%	17%	16%
Sometimes	52	60	52
Often	28	20	28
Almost always	7	3	4
	99%	100%	100%
N	(181)	(217)	(212)

greater inability to resist interruption than chemists do. Although the exact sources of this impression are unknown, the pattern is consistent with the hypothesis that routine in research is posively associated with immunity from doubts about personal adequacy.

Attributing difficulties and failures to factors beyond personal control is even less damaging to self-esteem than attributing them to a lack of motivation and effort. Individuals, it is argued, tend to attribute success to their personal abilities and dispositions, while crediting failure to unfavorable external conditions (Hastorf, *et. al.,* 1970:72-73). That scientific research is highly unroutinized entails great freedom in making judgments and attributing success or failure to various determinants (Glaser, 1964: Ch. 2, 4, 8, and 10).

This freedom is not without limit, however, and in fields with individualistic patterns of work it is difficult to protect self-esteem from failure by blaming it upon research instruments and subordinates. In this respect, research is probably personally more stressful in mathematics than in the empirical sciences, where fault may be laid at the door of instruments and subordinates. Table 3-18 shows that chemists and political scientists lay the blame for difficulties in their research on the lack of assistants and instruments more than do mathematicians. However, it may be that the higher proportions in chemistry and political science result simply from accurate perceptions of the importance of assistants and subordinates rather than from the assignment of blame to external factors. Since there is no objective evidence on the point, it is impossible to test this counterargument directly; nevertheless, an indirect test may be made by examining the evidence on lack of external support in greater detail. Insofar as the complaints are based upon accurate perceptions of the importance of assistants and instruments, one would expect them to decrease with increasing support, but not if they are simply evidence of the assignment of blame to external conditions.

Table 3-18.   **Frequency of Reports that Less Productive Periods are Caused by Lack of Assistants or Instruments, by Discipline**

		Discipline	
			Political
Frequency	Mathematics	Chemistry	Science
Never	92%	20%	49%
Sometimes	4	42	41
Often	4	38	10
	100%	100%	100%
N	(175)	(212)	(204)

Table 3-19 reports the percentage of respondents who blame lack of assistants or instruments for their less productive periods:[10]

Table 3-19.   **Percentages of Respondents Attributing Less Productive Periods to Need of Assistants or Instruments, by Number of Research Subordinates, and by Discipline**

Discipline	Number of Research Subordinates					
	0	1	2	3	4	5+
Mathematics	2%	0%	0%	0%	5%	25%
(N)	(49)	(34)	(41)	(17)	(19)	(20)
Chemistry	61%	35%	52%	53%	30%	27%
(N)	(18)	(23)	(30)	(32)	(23)	(89)
Political Science	13%	3%	10%	8%	19%	10%
(N)	(34)	(29)	(19)	(24)	(16)	(90)

Here chemists' charge that their difficulties in research result from the need of assistant or instruments is seen at least in part to be grounded in accurate perceptions; but this is not so in the case of political scientists. The findings are consistent with those presented in Table 3-9, namely, that among chemists there are substantially higher correlations between scholarly productivity and number of graduate students and postdoctoral fellows than among politi-

---

[10]This number is simply the sum of the numbers of graduate students, post-doctoral fellows and technicians that a scientist supervises either as a major professor or as an employer. Data concerning my respondents' use of various research instruments were not collected, and an examination of these complaints within categories of instrument use is therefore not possible.

cal scientists. Insofar as these correlations are measures of the objective impact of subordinates on productivity, they provide further evidence that the political scientists' statement that their difficulties in research result from lack of support are a manifestation of the misplacing of blame on external features of work rather than on personal deficiencies. Although mathematicians as a group rarely blame this circumstance, those with the most research subordinates cite it even more often than do political scientists. Once again, this pattern of responses and the results presented in Table 3-9 for mathematicians may reflect an improper assignment of blame; but the number of cases in the category in question is small. That subordinates and instruments provide possible alternative explanations which protect self-esteem from the vagaries of research may account at least in part for the fact that mathematicians, as opposed to chemists and political scientists, blame their difficulties on their own lack of ability.[11]

These comparisons between disciplines do no more than suggest some of the complex processes by which scientists come to terms with their work. Although they indicate the extent to which rather large differences in the organization and flow of research lead to differences in scientists' identification with their own efforts, the comparisons do not portray the dynamic adjustment and readjustment between work experience and perception of self. Even where personal failure is undeniable, a scientist may be able to maintain self-esteem and commitment to research by redefining both so as to minimize failure; repeated difficulties and failures in research work may result in a redefinition of self as a good teacher or as a sophisticated critic of the literature. When such redefinitions are effected, failure in research may cease because new peceptions of self alter the meaning of old performance.

In optimistic accounts of science the process of research is often in part portrayed as a process of discovering one's identity as an intellectual and a moral being (Weber, 1946:129-156; Schwartz and Schwartz, 1955; Sjoberg, 1967). Although it is usually assumed that the scientist can attain greater self-awareness through research, the contrary opinion is also commonly expressed. It is clear, however, that in the process of their research, scientists encounter many opportunities for redefining themselves in terms of work experiences.

Conclusion

When a scientist invests all his intellectual and psychological resources in one research topic, frustration can be disastrous (Stinchcombe, 1966:26). The ability to carry on research in several topics simultaneously is a function

---

[11]Among mathematicians, the correlation between the number of graduate students a scientist supervises and the extent to which the scientist attributes difficulties to his own lack of ability is $-.26$ (N $=$ 173). The latter measure was constructed by assigning values to the categories in Table 3-16 ("never" $= 0$, "often" $= 2$), and the sloppiness of this measure greatly attenuates its correlation with the number of graduate students supervised. Although this correlation could arise from a variety of sources, it is consistent with the expectation that mathematicians would be able to blame others for difficulties in research more often if in fact there were more people there to blame.

of routine; when a scholar's research is highly unroutinized, progress typically requires constant attention, and preoccupation with one research problem precludes work on others. Evidence supporting these two propositions (but not one in contradistinction to the other) is provided by responses to a question I asked the scientists in my samples about concurrent research on more than one topic (Table 3-20). They reveal that chemists tend to carry on research in several questions simultaneously to a greater extent than do mathematicians or political scientists, and this is probably both a consequence and a cause of the more extensive routine in research in chemistry. Thus routine forms or work tend to be self-sustaining because of both the long-range and the day-to-day adaptations which they make possible.

The degree of routine which characterizes research in a given field and the various adaptations that scientists make in order to produce research may be associated with a host of other behavioral patterns not specific to performance. Stereotypes of the dress and demeanor of scientists in different disciplines are accepted because of general belief that those who perform unroutinized work are to be granted freedom from convention. The abstract and irrational nature of research in mathematics is supposedly expressed in modes of dress and patterns of behavior which feature corresponding eccentricities; social scientists are supposedly verbose and socially aggressive, and chemists, whose work entails more routine than any of the three fields,

Table 3-20.   Practices in Simultaneously Investigating More Than One Problem, by Discipline

	Discipline		
Usual Practice	**Mathematics**	**Chemistry**	**Political Science**
I usually focus my attention on only one particular research question at a time	15%	4%	12%
At a given time I am usually investigating one primary question, although I do a little work on a few others	56	20	43
I usually carry on investigations of two or three main questions simultaneously	24	61	36
I usually carry on investigations of more than three main questions simultaneously	5	15	9
	100%	100%	100%
N	(182)	(218)	(212)

supposedly are the most conventional.[12] One would expect of chemists greater religious and political orthodoxy, higher rates of marriage and lower rates of divorce, and the like, than of mathematicians or political scientists (Ladd and Lipset, 1972; and Hudson and Jacot, 1971). Although such stereotypes are grossly overdrawn, they illustrate connections between work and behavior constructed from casual observation. Just as a greater understanding of the meaning and motivation of an individual's behavior may be gained by knowing what kind of work he does, so an understanding of the nature of various kinds of work may come from systematically examining typical differences in the behavior patterns of the actors.

---

[12]Such differences have been interpreted traditionally as manifestations of psychological differences among men typically selected into various academic disciplines. For example, see Roe (1953).

CHAPTER 4

SOURCES OF ROUTINE IN SCIENTIFIC RESEARCH

In the preceding chapter, routine in research was seen as associated with the sharing of efficacious techniques; no attempt was made to analyze the sources of the relationship between the two. Discussion of the nature of the relationship between technique and routine in science tends to take one of two forms: First, the two features are often seen as consequences of the cognitive content of the given field and as intimately related to the sharing of more general paradigms or theories about the phenomena chosen for investigation (Kuhn, 1961). In general, one would expect fields where there is little consensus on theoretical issues to lack both efficacious techniques and extensive routine. Second, certain characteristics of research techniques are often said to have an independent effect on the routine of research which cannot be accounted for by mutual dependence upon consensus on theoretical issues. For example, it is alleged that in recent times generally strong support of scientific activities has fostered the development of new techniques for the mass production of data. The high cost and complexity of the new instruments have supposedly brought about major changes in the pattern and pace of research work; in particular, in the routinization and bureaucratization of scientific research and its subsequent trivialization.

Routine and Patterns of Normative Integration

There is good reason to believe that some sort of agreement on the appropriate problems and techniques of research in a given field is a necessary condition of relatively extensive routine in it. In contrast to many other kinds of work in industrial societies, scientific research is unique in the extent to which workers, rather than employers or clients, collectively control the social mechanisms by which the goals and means of the work are defined, and by which rewards for successful performance are assigned. As a result, the amount of routine in research in a given field is at least in part a function of the extent to which research workers share beliefs about appropriate goals, methods, and standards. Where they do not agree on these things their efforts are not guided by common conceptions of research problems and methods for their solution. Moreover, they are not able to predict each other's evaluations of their solutions. Under these conditions, research workers are likely to perceive their efforts as other than routine.

It is more difficult to specify the conditions which are sufficient for the development of relatively extensive routine. Kuhn argues that research in "mature" or "paradigmatic" scientific communities is likely to be relatively routine in comparison with that in fields which are experiencing preparadigmatic, multi-paradigmatic or extraordinary science (Masterman, 1970: 73-75). An examination of this question, and of the prerequisites of normal science may illustrate some of the difficulties met in specifying the preconditions of a high degree of routine.

Kuhn has characterized normal science as a puzzle-solving activity, stressing two characteristics of puzzles which are particularly relevant to research questions (1964:38). First, puzzles are problems which are assumed to have solutions; scientists can be confident that their research questions are not nonsensical artifacts of erroneous theories. Second, puzzles have rules that limit both the nature of acceptable solutions and the steps by which they are obtained. With respect to research, this implies that scientists share "rules" about the conditions under which research questions will be judged to have been answered, and the techniques of investigation which may be employed.[1] The permitted techniques are presumed to be sufficient for the attainment of agreed-upon answers even though, at times, the individual researcher worker finds himself unable to marshal them effectively.

Scientists are unlikely to remain adherents of a given normal-science tradition when their assumptions about the existence and nature of answers to questions, and the techniques for obtaining them are cast in doubt by persistent failure. On the other hand, fairly regular success in obtaining solutions is one condition under which they will perceive their assumptions as justified. Thus normal science is associated with success in obtaining acceptable answers to research questions.

These characteristics of normal science resemble the two criteria of routine (Chapter 3): disruptions of work are few and workers can make effective adaptations to them. Although these conditions are rarely present in scientific research, they can be used in identifying *relatively* routine forms. Accordingly, research is routine when research workers' efforts regularly yield answers which are perceived to be "successful" or "adequate," and when

---

[1]Consistent with Kuhn's usage, the term "rule" is used here in a broader sense than that which restricts it to explicit injunctions (Kuhn, 1964: 38-39).

the workers agree on what techniques of investigation are appropriate and what modifications of them are allowable when no adequate answer is reached.

Of course, Kuhn's discussion of normal science involves more elements than those named in this statement of his puzzle-solving analogy. For example, he reasons that a particular normal science tradition must be sufficiently open-ended as to leave all sorts of problems for future resolution (1964:10). Kuhn's criteria of normal science and the characteristics of routine work are certainly not the same; nevertheless, it is reasonable to assert that the characteristics of routine are included among his criteria of normal science and therefore that research in scientific communities characterized by normal science is likely to be relatively routine in comparison to research in fields which are in a extraordinary, pre-paradigmatic, or multi-paradigmatic state. Indeed, those who object to Kuhn's advocacy of the indispensability of normal science to scientific progress often do so on the ground that normal science is an uninteresting, uncritical, and routine activity which threatens the flexibility and creativity necessary to the fundamental innovations upon which scientific progress depends (Popper, 1970). Such objections rely heavily on the pejorative connotation of routine and overlook both the logical and psychological necessity of at least some stability in patterns of creative activity.[2]

Given that normal science is characterized by relatively extensive routine in research, the sufficient conditions of normal science are also those of the development of high levels of routine. Originally Kuhn attributed the presence of normal science in a given scientific community to the sharing by the members of a paradigm. Although he used the term "paradigm" in a variety of ways,[3] in the most general sense he meant a "constellation of beliefs, values, techniques, and so on" concerning the performance of research work in the given community (1970:175). He made it clear that a paradigm is the "fundamental unit of analysis for the student of scientific development, a unit that cannot be reduced to logically atomic components which might function in its stead" (1964:11). The sharing of a paradigm is therefore closely related to the idea of normative integration discussed in Chapter 2.

This kind of argument introduces an immediate difficulty. If the sharing of a paradigm leads to normal science and relatively routine research work, then it follows that the fields with a high component of nonroutine must not share a paradigm. Since, as already noted, research work in mathematics is highly unroutinized, it is implied that mathematicians do not share a paradigm. But this seems to contradict the evidence presented in Chapter 2 showing that mathematics is relatively highly integrated normatively—and also

---

[2]Kuhn (1970b:233) has pointed out the logical necessity of stability in demarcating change in science. The psychological advantages of some routine in otherwise non-routine work such as scientific research were discussed in Chapter 3 of this work.

[3]Masterman (1970:61-65) lists 21 senses in which the term "paradigm" is used in *The Structure of Scientific Revolutions*, and tries to group the various usages into three general categories. Another discussion of Kuhn's imprecision in defining the concept of a paradigm, and of some results of it, has been presented by Shapere (1971).

Kuhn's assertion about the prehistoric origins of paradigms in mathematics (1964:15).

More recently, Kuhn has modified his original formulation so that it no longer gives rise to this difficulty.[4] First, he abandoned his earlier position that the presence of a paradigm is a sufficient condition of normal science:

> The nature of [the] transition to maturity deserves fuller discussion than it has received in this book, particularly from those concerned with the development of the contemporary social sciences. To that end it may help to point out that the transition need not (I now think should not) be associated with the first acquisition of a paradigm. The members of all scientific communities, including the schools of the "pre-paradigm" period, share the sorts of elements which I have collectively labelled "a paradigm." What changes with the transition to maturity is not the presence of a paradigm but rather its nature. Only after the change is normal puzzle-solving research possible. Many of the attributes of a developed science which I [earlier] associated with the acquisition of a paradigm I would therefore now discuss as consequences of the acquisition of the sort of paradigm that identifies challenging puzzles, supplies clues to their solution, and guarantees that the truly clever practitioner will succeed (1970:178-179).

Second, Kuhn took steps to specify the elements of shared commitment which constitute a paradigm. Thus he now describes a paradigm as a "disciplinary matrix," which "is composed of ordered elements of various sorts, each requiring further specification."

> All or most of the objects of group commitment that my original text makes paradigms, parts of paradigms, or paradigmatic are constituents of the disciplinary matrix, and as such they form a whole and function together. They are, however, no longer to be discussed as though they were all of a piece (1970a:182).

In a preliminary list of the elements of a disciplinary matrix, he includes symbolic generalizations, metaphysical and heuristic models, general values (such as the belief that a theory should possess internal and external logical consistency), and exemplary concrete problem solutions, which he refers to as exemplars (1970:181-191).

By taking these steps, Kuhn hoped to eliminate some of the ambiguities and circularities of his original formulation, and, above all, to discourage interpretation of a paradigm as "a quasi-mystical entity that, like charisma, transforms those infected by it" (1970b:272). His reformulation points up the possibility that there may be disparities in the sharing, by the members of a field, of the various elements of a paradigm (Ben David, 1964:470-476). Thus, mathematicians may strongly agree on the importance of various research problems, and on the standards by which their solutions will be judged, even though they do not share efficacious techniques for producing formal proofs. As a result, research in mathematics may be highly unroutinized, even though mathematicians in general agree on most of the elements of a paradigm.

---

[4]This is not to say that Kuhn modified his position in order to resolve the particular problem noted here. See Kuhn (1970a:174-210) for an account of his reasons for his reformulations.

In cases where agreement is confined to only one or two of the elements of a possible paradigm one might speak of "incomplete paradigms" or "paradigm fragments."[5] For example, Masterman claims that in the contemporary social sciences:

> . . . each sub-field as defined by its technique is so obviously more trivial and narrow than the field as defined by intuition, and also the various operational definitions given by the techniques are so grossly discordant with one another, that discussion on fundamentals remains and long-run progress (as opposed to local progress) fails to occur (1970:74).

Accordingly, one might characterize the contemporary social sciences as consisting of a multiplicity of paradigm fragments, some being primarily techniques without concomitant theoretical models and generalizations, others being metaphysical models without implied research techniques or concrete predictions, and still others being focused upon apparently trivial and narrow (in the sense discussed by Masterman) substantive topics. It should be noted that this characterization of paradigms in the social sciences is consistent with Hagstrom's observation that social scientists are eclectic about the paradigms in their fields rather than committed to any one of them (1964: 195).[6] When paradigms are incomplete, they do not stimulate that commitment prerequisite of vehement disagreement and strenuous competition between the members of existing "schools."

By breaking paradigms down into constituent elements, Kuhn throws open questions about the relations of the elements to each other, and the extent to which they must be internally consistent and complete before they can support a normal science tradition (Shapere, 1971:707). Although the most dramatic instances of scientific revolution and the emergence of new normal science tradition may involve paradigms which inspire a uniformly high degree of consensus on questions of theory, problem identification, method, and so on, the consensus on the various elements of a paradigm should be empirically questioned rather than assumed as equal. And because of the possibility that the various elements may inspire different degrees of consensus, a perfect association between the amount of routine in a field and overall measures of its normative integration cannot be assumed.

Paradigms and Predictability

Whatever the logical and philosophical reasons for Kuhn's reformulation of his original statements on the relations between paradigms and normal

---

[5]Masterman (1970:73-77) has pointed out some of the similarities of Kuhn's view of science and earlier hypothetico-deductive views, but she does not phrase her discussion of "pre-paradigmatic" science in a manner similar to hypothetico-deductive accounts of such science. The idea of an "incomplete paradigm" or a "paradigm fragment" is functionally equivalent to Hempel's concept of an "explanation sketch;" both attempt to characterize the features which distinguish the "hard" from the "soft" sciences. See Hempel (1965:231-243).

[6]In contrast, Masterman (1970:74) and Kuhn (1970a:162-163, 179) postulate that social scientists are organized into a multiplicity of communities, each around a distinct paradigm. This leads them to an apparently exaggerated estimation of social commitment and conflict in the social sciences.

science, one wonders if the original formulation is inconsistent with any empirical evidence other than that presented above in connection with routine in research in mathematics. If this is the only instance of what appears to be a disparity in the sharing of the various possible elements of a paradigm, then perhaps the reformulation has little empirical significance and one can say that, except in mathematics, routine in research is determined by the field's normative integration. On the other hand, if other instances can be discovered it might justify greater confidence that Kuhn's reformulation has empirical significance. Interestingly enough, evidence of another instance of possible disparity in the sharing of different elements of a paradigm is contained in a recent demonstration of the validity of Kuhn's original discussion of the relations between normal science and paradigm-sharing.

In the only systematic discussion of relationships between a discipline's solidarity and scientists' work experiences published to date, Lodahl and Gordon (1972) tested the hypothesis that fields with highly developed paradigms are also characterized by highly predictable activities. Following Kuhn, Lodahl and Gordon begin by defining a paradigm has a constellation of shared beliefs about the nature of some set of phenomena and about the manner in which the phenomena should be studied.

> The scientific paradigm . . . includes not only the accepted theory and findings of the field, but also the preferred methodologies, the tacit understandings over those areas considered important to study, etc. The paradigm provides structure by suggesting which problems next require investigation, what methods are appropriate to their study, and even which findings are indeed "proven." Following from this, the essence of the paradigm concept is the degree of consensus or sharing of beliefs within a scientific field about theory, methodology, techniques, and problems (1972:57-58).

At this point, however, Lodahl and Gordon depart from Kuhn's recent discussions of the concept. Instead of allowing for the possibility that a paradigm may be a loose assemblage of elements not necessarily integrated into a coherent whole, they discuss paradigms only as unitary entities which are, in some sense, more or less developed. This is implied by such statements as "These definitions suggest that paradigms largely determine the technology of scientific fields, not only in the methods that are employed, but also in the more general sense of predictability or certainly of technology" (1972:50). Thus, rather than viewing preferred "technologies" as one element in a scientific paradigm, Lodahl and Gordon see them as a result of an existing paradigm.

Lodahl and Gordon postulate a "continuum of degrees of scientific development in terms of paradigm development," rather than treating scientific development as a set of discrete stages along the lines suggested by Kuhn. For lack of a more felicitous phraseology, they refer to fields with well-developed paradigms as "high-paradigm fields" and to fields with poorly developed paradigms as "low-paradigm fields." In order to determine degree of paradigm development, they employ two measures: rankings of the maturity or development of various disciplines made by scientists in a subset of those disciplines, and measures of the perceived agreement among scientists in several fields on the appropriate content of their undergraduate and graduate curricula. That these are seen as measures of a general characteristic of a discipline rather than as measures of specific elements of a paradigm is clearly spelled out in a discussion of agreement over curricula as a measure of paradigm development.

> Since paradigm level is defined by the amount of agreement over theory, methodology, etc., we should find indicators of high agreement within fields designated as having high paradigm development, and relatively less agreement in fields designated as having low paradigm development. Such agreement should be evident in the most general aspects of the teaching curriculum, those instances where the objective was to cover all of the important content of the field. A highly developed paradigm with the associated consensus should thus be reflected in high agreement over the content of survey courses, and also in the requirements and content of graduate programs (1972:60).

Consistent with their expectations, the authors find that by these measures the two natural sciences in their study, physics and chemistry, have high paradigm development, while their two social sciences, sociology and political science, have low paradigm development.

Lodahl and Gordon's discussion of the concept of "predictability" is more sketchy than their interpretation of the idea of a paradigm. In their first presentation of the hypothesis that predictability is positively related to paradigm development, they state:

> When scientists in a field have large areas of agreement over both scientific goals and means, there is a high probability of certain courses of action. In a sense those activities are predictable (1972: 58).

That predictability is interpreted broadly as a high probability of certain courses of action is also evident in a more detailed discussion of their reasons for believing that paradigm development should be related to predictability.

> The high consensus found in high-paradigm fields enhances predictability in at least two ways: (1) it provides an accepted and shared vocabulary for discussing the content of the field; and (2) it provides an accumulation of detailed information (scientific findings) on what has been successful in the past. The advantages in superior communication process and superior information inventory should be evident in all scientific tasks that involve communication and decision-making (1972:61).

The greater predictability hypothesized of fields with developed paradigms is therefore to be manifested in a variety of scientists' tasks and experiences, from among which Lodahl and Gordon studied two main groups: those associated with teaching, and those associated with research. In the first group, they investigated among scientists in various fields:

(1) Satisfaction with their teaching of graduate students as intellectually stimulating work, and desire for more time with them.
(2) Use of teaching assistants in their courses.
(3) Desire for more teaching assistants.

In the second group they studied:

(1) Disagreement with research collaborators.
(2) Number of research assistants.
(3) Desire for more research assistants.
(4) Willingness to assist graduate students on their theses and research.

Although Lodahl and Gordon's broad specification of predictability as a "high probability of certain courses of action" is more general than the criteria of routine outlined above, it is reasonable to conclude that the concepts of predictability and routine are closely related (Perrow, 1967:196-197; Litwak, 1961:177-179). This is apparent, for example, in Lodahl and Gordon's contention that the scientist's use of research assistants and graduate students in his research is an indication of the predictability of his research activities —a viewpoint consistent with the discussion of the division of labor presented in the previous chapter.

On the other hand, since the work reported above was concerned exclusively with research, I have not considered the possible determinants of routine characteristic of teaching in various fields. Lodahl and Gordon argue that paradigm development determines the predictability of both research and teaching, and they imply that across fields relative routine in research is strongly correlated with relative routine in teaching. Both these ideas follow from the authors' holistic conception: instead of entertaining the possibility that various characteristics of a scientific paradigm may determine the routine of teaching as opposed to research, they tend to assume that a paradigm is a unitary entity whose consequences are uniform reflections of its current state. There is evidence, however, that teaching and research in certain disciplines differ greatly in extent of routine.

On the basis of my earlier discussion, one might expect in mathematics a large disparity between routine in teaching and that in research. I have already established that research in mathematics is relatively not routine, at least in comparison to research in chemistry and political science, the lack of routine being attributed to the lack of efficacious techniques for producing formal proof. On the other hand, one would expect the relative consensus on standards of proof found in mathematics to facilitate instruction, since the students' primary task is to assimilate past achievements, not to initiate new ones.

Unfortunately, Lodahl and Gordon did not include mathematics among the disciplines they studied, and information about the relative routine of teaching was not collected for the three fields included in the study reported here. Such information is available, however, in work previously reported by Bernard Berelson (1960). Berelson asked a sample of graduate faculty members at American universities: "By and large, how would you say you and your colleagues feel about the state of graduate training in your field at your institution?" Although phrased more broadly, this question appears to tap the same sentiments as those tapped by the first of the three questions used by Lodahl and Gordon to determine the predictability of teaching activities. Following those authors, one would expect teaching to be most fruitful and rewarding in fields characterized by relative consensus. If this reasoning is correct, and if the extent of routine in teaching is positively correlated with routine in research, one should find relatively less routine in the teaching of mathematics as measured by responses to Berelson's question.

Berelson (1960:204-205) reported the proportion of respondents in a variety of fields who were dissatisfied with their graduate training program, and his findings are reproduced in Table 4-1 for the five fields included in the present study and the study reported by Lodahl and Gordon.[7]

Contrary to expectations based on the assumption of a positive relationship between routine in teaching and that in research, Table 4-1 shows mathematicians as the least dissatisfied with their training of graduates. If, as argued above, this may be taken as evidence that teaching activities are relatively predictable or routine in mathematics, then the argument that routine in both teaching and research is determined by some overall level of "paradigm development" appears questionable. The alternative argument, that it is necessary to conceive of scientific paradigms as consisting of discrete and potentially malintegrated elements with various elements or combinations of elements affecting diverse types of work experiences, is acceptable.

A tendency to treat paradigms, and the kinds of scientific work they support, in a holistic fashion is also shown by Lodahl and Gordon's reaction to unexpected findings they uncover when looking at their measures of the

Table 4-1. **Proportions of Graduate Faculty Reporting Dissatisfaction With Graduate Training at Their Institutions, by Discipline**

Discipline	Proportion Dissatisfied
Mathematics and statistics	.32
Physics	.34
Chemistry	.36
Sociology	.48
Political Science	.48

[7]Berelson failed to report the number of cases upon which each field's proportion is based, but aggregate information which he presents about some of the characteristics of his samples (1960:276) suggests that samples of each field consist of slightly less than 100 cases. He gives results for mathematics and statistics combined, since academic statisticians are often found in departments of mathematics, but in view of the small numbers of statisticians probably involved, and the similarities in teaching patterns in mathematics and academic statistics, the combination probably doesn't yield results which differ from those for mathematicians alone. It should also be noted that Lodahl and Gordon's rankings of satisfaction with teaching activities in physics and chemistry on the one hand, and sociology and political science, on the other, replicate Berelson's.

predictability of research in physics. All their measures of the use of research assistants and graduate students, as well as of the desire for more of the same, show physicists to be less "predictable" (i.e., to have fewer assistants and to desire no more of them) than chemists. Indeed, in many instances physicists, in their desire for and use of assistants in research, are similar to sociologists and political scientists.

On the basis of these results and the assumptions of a uniform level of consensus on the various elements of a paradigm and of a high level of consensus as sufficient for normal science, Lodahl and Gordon conclude that modern physics is going through a crisis. The conclusion itself, however, appears to be of doubtful validity. First, it seems to be contradicted by evidence which the authors themselves present, that both physicists and chemists disagree less among themselves when they are collaborating on research projects than do sociologists or political scientists (1972:63). If physics were indeed in crisis, one would expect such disagreement to be much more prominent than appears from these results. Second, there seems to be a contradiction between maintaining, on the one hand, that physics is a "high-paradigm" discipline, characterized by a great consensus as to the goals and means of scientific work, and, on the other, claiming that physics is going through crisis or a period of extraordinary science.

These difficulties would have been avoided had the authors not made inferences about the overall state of the paradigm of modern physics on the basis of information about physicists' utilization of and desire for various kinds of assistants in their research. Unfortunately, their desire to demonstrate a one-to-one correspondence between paradigm development and routine appears to have blinded them to alternative explanations of routine in research in physics; for example, that differences in the work patterns of experimental and theoretical physicists may account for their unexpected results. Research in physics shows great differentiation between theoretical and empirical work (Gamow, 1966:139-140) manifested in striking differences in typical work patterns (Gaston, 1973:26-31). One would expect work patterns in theoretical physics to be relatively unroutinized in comparison to those in experimental physics, and that theoretical physicists would resemble mathematicians in their use of research assistants more than they resemble experimental physicists. This is demonstrated by the use of graduate students and technicians found in samples of scientists in the two branches of physics. Corresponding data, reproduced below from a report by Hagstrom, were also collected for a formal science, mathematics, and other natural sciences, chemistry and experimental biology (1967:122).

As expected, patterns of the use of assistants in theoretical physics are more similar to those in mathematics than in experimental physics and the other empirical sciences in the table. Further evidence is present in responses given to Hagstrom, who asked his respondents how satisfied they were with the amount of assistance they had for their research. Forty-eight percent of the mathematicians and twenty percent of the theoretical physicists reported that they neither had nor wanted assistants. In comparison, the corresponding percentages in experimental physics, chemistry, and experimental biology were, respectively, zero percent, two percent, and one percent (1967:123).

Thus, Lodahl and Gordon's demonstration that physicists, on the whole, use research assistants less than do chemists, and in about the same measure as do, for instance, sociologists and political scientists, may be explained by the fact that the two branches of physics encompass very different patterns of research work. Research in theoretical physics resembles that in the formal sciences, and it has already been shown that mathematics uses fewer assistants than do even "low paradigm" social sciences. But research in experimental physics resembles that in other natural sciences, where greater numbers of assistants are needed. When the use of research assistants is examined in theoretical and experimental physics combined, it is not surprising that an aggregate level is found which is close to that in the social sciences. Rather than interpreting the aggregate level as evidence that physics is going through a period of extraordinary science or a crisis, it therefore seems more reasonable to attribute it to the diverse types of research in physics.

In summary, there appears reason to doubt the hypothesis of a close relationship in scientific disciplines between measures of routine and normative integration. Variation in routine in the various activities within a discipline suggests that scientific paradigms may be made up of elements which are not all accepted to the same extent. As a result, inferences about overall normative integration, if based only on information about the routine in particular activities, are highly suspect. In the case of physics, for example, the limited use of assistants in research is probably a result of the mathematical formalization of theory and the presence of scientists who specialize in theoretical work, rather than of a major decline in normative integration in the discipline as a whole.[8] All this is not to imply that there is no relation between the normative integration in a given field and the routine of its various activities. It seems reasonable to argue that no great amount of routine can exist in fields with little consensus on the various elements of a paradigm. But until we have a better model of these elements and of their relations to scientists' various tasks, inferences about levels of consensus based upon information about routine in the various activities must be highly tentative.

Routine and Technological Transformations of Research

Many who have commented upon recent transformations of American academic science claim that new techniques made possible by high-level support tend to routinize research. "Big" science is alleged to be routine science; moreover, the routinization which is part of big science is often viewed as a threat to fundamental norms and values. It has been stated, for example, that the increased technical and organizational capacity to produce mere "information" as opposed to "knowledge" leads scientists to lose sight of

---

[8]It does not seem reasonable to argue that the differentiation of theorists and experimentalists in physics is a consequence of the hypothesized state of crisis in physics. Instead, it is probably, as Gamow claims, a result of the mathematization of physical theory. Nor does it seem reasonable to argue that the mathematization of theory is a reflection of crisis.

the crucial distinction between them, and of the central principles and problems of their disciplines (Weiss, 1971:127-137). This is to argue that the routinization of the process of research brings about the trivialization of its products and substitutes a dogmatic for a curious and critical spirit. Scientists, then, are said to adopt the perspective of the engineer and to apply learned techniques mechanically instead of imaginatively (Popper, 1970:52-53). If this is true, then routine in scientific research is a symptom of the intellectual disorganization of science, not a sign of its intellectual integration.

Discussions of the impact of modern research techniques upon contemporary research tend to be wide-ranging polemics rather than carefully constructed arguments. However, there are two lines of argument to explain how recently developed techniques come to routinize and trivialize research. First, the costliness and complexity of modern research instruments may lead to the decline of traditional patterns of the organization of work, the free collaboration of peers and the supervision of graduate students by professors, and to the rise of more hierarchical bureaucratic patterns. When the costs of constructing and operating research instruments are high, and their operation requires a variety of specialists, individualistic patterns are supplanted by collective ones. The forces which lead to this transformation are the same as those which have led to the replacement of free partnership and apprenticeship by the modern corporation: individuals themselves cannot provide the massive financial resources which are needed, and the new patterns of organization offer competitive advantages over the old.[9]

Unfortunately, bureaucratic patterns of organization presuppose specificity in the goals and means of the work, but scientific research is not amenable to the specification of goals and means. It is often stated that there is an inherent tension between the demand for order and predictability in bureaucratic forms of research organization and the need for flexibility and creativity if science is to advance. Thus the increased use of complex research techniques is held to have brought about changes in the organization of research; and the new patterns are said to foster the inappropriate routinization and trivialization of research (Whyte, 1956:239-253).

Second, it is argued that the increased sophistication and complexity of modern research instruments leads to overemphasis on method and a corresponding neglect of substantive considerations. These tendencies, epitomized by the emergence of the "professional technician"—the Ph.D. who operates equipment and gives technical advice to research workers but who does no research of his own (Hagstrom, 1964b:253-255)—are alleged to be especially prominent among recently trained scientists. More complex techniques of research have made it necessary for academic scientists to gather about them more and more subordinates and to set up among them a stricter division

---

[9]The competitive advantages of modern over traditional forms of scientific teamwork are noted much less often than the association between the modern forms and the costliness and complexity of the instruments of research. This difference is consistent with the general view that modern forms of scientific teamwork are imposed upon scientists by external forces rather than actively sought out by them. For an example of the competitive advantages of modern forms, see Klaw (1968:143-144).

of labor. Graduate students trained under these conditions may attain great technical proficiency but their education is so narrow that they often reach the doctorate without an understanding either of the research enterprise as a whole or of the distinction between important and trivial topics. Weiss describes this condition:

> We see instruments turning from servants into tyrants, forcing the captive scientist to mass-produce and market senseless data beyond the point of conceivable usefulness—a modern version of the Sorcerer's Apprentice. We see bewildered youngsters composing research projects like abstract paintings: picking some colorful and fashionable words from recent literature, and then reshuffling and recombining them into another conglomerate, yielding a stew of data, both undigested and indigestible. We see narrow specialists lavishing their pet technique on reconfirming in yet another dozen ways what has already been superabundantly established to everybody's satisfaction. But why go on? Most of you know the hallmarks of this growing dilution of our research effectiveness. They are irrelevance, triviality, redundancy, lack of perspective, and an unbounded flair for proliferation (Weiss, 1971:113-114).

This is a restatement of Mannheim's pronouncement that industrialization and the division of labor rob the worker of his insight into the nature and consequences of his efforts, and bring about an increase in the functional rationality of activities and individuals, but not to an increase in their substantial rationality (Mannheim, 1940:51-60).

Rigorous tests of these arguments would require time-series data on the variables involved, and, unfortunately, such are not available. Cross-sectional measures of some of the variables are at hand from a variety of scientific fields, however, making it possible to check elements of the arguments with them. Included are such fields as mathematics and theoretical physics which can serve as baselines of comparison for other fields which have been subject to the technological developments discussed above.

Technological Development and the Bureaucratization of Science

If the consequences of new, expensive and complex research instruments are the increased coordination of scientific research and therefore the increased prominence of organizations such as research centers and institutes, one would expect to find in fields where such instruments are extensively used a relatively greater importance of formal organization. In his study of competition and teamwork in science, Hagstrom asked his respondents whether they were currently using a number of recently developed techniques or instruments in their research, including among them electronic digital computers, radioactive tracers, electron microscopes, vapor-phase chromatography, nuclear magnetic resonance spectroscopy, infrared spectroscopy, ultraviolet spectroscopy, electron-spin resonance spectroscopy, mass spectroscopy, and subatomic particle accelerators.[10] This list certainly does not allow the precise ranking of fields in terms of the average number of techniques used in them; in particular, it appears to overrepresent techniques

---

[10]Further information about these techniques, and their implications for the size of the research groups which use them, is contained in Hagstrom (1967:30-34).

Table 4-2.   **Use of Subordinates, by Discipline**

Number of Subordinates		Mathematics	Theoretical Physics	Experimental Physics	Chemistry	Experimental Biology
1. Number of graduate students working full- or part-time	Mean	1.59	2.35	3.58	4.02	3.07
	S.D.	2.57	1.28	2.87	3.28	3.17
	(N)	(281)	(156)	(292)	(517)	(319)
2. Number of technicians working at least half-time	Mean	.35	.27	2.07	.64	1.64
	S.D.	2.12	.86	3.52	1.61	1.71
	(N)	(282)	(155)	(292)	(512)	(319)

that are used primarily by chemists. However, a rough indication of the use of recently developed techniques in each field is the proportion of scientists who use *none* of those listed.[11] These proportions are reported in panel A, Table 4-3, in nine specific specialties studied by Hagstrom. As one would expect, the general areas of experimental physics, chemistry, and experimental biology show greater use of these new techniques than do theoretical physics, mathematics and statistics, and "other biology."[12]

Hagstrom also asked his respondents about participation in various patterns of collaboration (Panel B, Table 4-3). Actually, these arrangements are not mutually exclusive: for example, about a third of those reporting collaboration with colleagues in formal institutions and centers in the various fields included in Table 4-3 also collaborated with others outside their organizations. My purposes in combining all such workers into this single category was to obtain an estimate of the upper limit of the proportion in each field whose research involved collaboration within a single formal research organization.

Hagstrom (1967:25-26, 41-46; 1964b:241-263) has noted that, regardless of the extent to which recent transformations of research may have forced scientists to coordinate their work, traditional teamwork is still dominant. Except for experimental nuclear physicists, at least 50 percent of the scientists in each specialty in Table 4-3 either did not collaborate or did so only

---

[11]Actually, these proportions rank the fields in Table 4-3 in more or less the same order as the median number of techniques used by the scientists in each field. Thus the results described below hold for either index of the use of complex and expensive techniques.

[12]Included in the general category of scientists in "experimental biology" are respondents from departments of molecular biology, bacteriology, applied microbiology, plant physiology, physiology and genetics. "Other biology" includes members of departments of botony, zoology, anatomy, ecology, and a few scientists in clinical fields. For more detailed information on the composition of these two general groups, see Hagstrom (1967:91-94).

Table 4-3. Use of Modern Techniques in Research and Prevalence of Scientific Teamwork, by Specialty

	Mathematics and Statistics	Theoretical Physics	Experimental Nuclear Physics	Experimental Solid State Physics	Other Experimental Physics	Physical Chemistry	Inorganic and Organic Chemistry	Experimental Biology	Other Biology
A. Percent of Scientists who are currently using none of the listed instruments and techniques	74%	52%	5%	20%	21%	11%	8%	27%	45%
N	(192)	(119)	(81)	(61)	(78)	(185)	(191)	(247)	(122)
B. Percent of Scientists who:									
1. Collaborate with colleagues in research centers or institutes	9%	17%	37%	14%	18%	11%	3%	18%	15%
2. Collaborate with colleagues on funded research	12	19	33	15	32	8	13	19	18
3. Collaborate informally (not on funded research)	26	27	15	20	16	26	28	23	30
4. Do not collaborate with colleagues of faculty rank or equivalent status in research	53	37	15	51	34	55	56	40	37
Total	100%	100%	100%	100%	100%	100%	100%	100%	100%
N	(195)	(121)	(79)	(61)	(79)	(184)	(202)	(250)	(122)

SPECIALTY

informally. Even those who were collaborating on funded research should probably be classified as engaged in a traditional form of scientific team-work since these are often only transitory arrangements which endure only as long as the grant lasts. Thus the best indicator of the bureaucratization of scientific research in the various specialties shown in Table 4-3 is the percent who reported collaboration with colleagues in research institutes or centers; and again, except for experimental nuclear physics, these percentages are fairly small.

Large differences in the use of complex and expensive techniques, such as the difference between experimental solid-state physics and theoretical physics, or the difference between inorganic chemistry and mathematics and statistics, are not associated with the rather small variations in collabora-tion within formal research organizations. Thus there is no strong link be-tween the use of such techniques and the decline of traditional forms of scientific teamwork.

Although these results might at first seem surprising, two considerations may lessen the force of the original arguments linking new research tech-niques and the proliferation of bureaucratic research organizations: First norms of individualism and autonomy are strong among academic scientists, and when they are forced to become members of hierarchical research or-ganizations in order to take advantage of new techniques, there will usually be pressure either to "democratize" the techniques, or to place them in service organizations which will minister to scientists' individual needs. Cases in point are mass spectroscopy and digital computers. Originally these tools were sufficiently complex to require trained specialists, and this in turn probably fostered the development of larger and more hierarchical organizations. More recently, however, patterns of access to these tools have changed. In the case of mass spectroscopy, machinery has been devel-oped which may be operated by the average scientist and which is within his financial means (for additional examples, see Committee for the Survey of Chemistry, 1965:92-102). In the case of computers, service organizations and simple standardized means have been set up by which the scientist can do his own programming.[13] Both developments have led to a decline in the demand for technical specialists and therefore to the restoration of tra-ditional arrangements in teamwork.

Second, the original arguments appear to overestimate the extent to which modern forms, such as research centers and institutes, are based upon bureaucratic principles of organization. We have only a few descriptions of research in such organizations, and these tend to focus on the most hier-

---

[13]Although this is the primary mode of the adaptation of computers, recent years have also seen the development of small special-purpose computers that are within individual scientists' financial means. Transformations similar to those of large compu-ters have also been noted in astronomy and high-energy nuclear physics. Scientists who developed larger and more complex types of telescopes and particle accelerators in order to carry out research originally had to cooperate in their construction and maintenance. There is a tendency, however, for maintenance functions to be assigned to service bureaucracies whose functions are similar to those of the modern computer center (Klaw, 1968:150-151).

archical, such as the Lawrence Radiation Laboratories at the University of California (Hagstrom, 1965:143-147; Klaw, 1968:136-139; Swatez, 1970). But even there the individual scientist often enjoys considerable autonomy and power. Taken as a whole, modern research organizations probably resemble medieval guilds as much as capitalist firms or complex bureaucracies. This is especially true with respect to their internal patterns of authority, the diffuse nature of their goals, and the functions they perform in obtaining and maintaining support from without. In any case, their emergence is often not in response to a need for the rational and efficient operation of complex and expensive new research techniques, and they are rarely structured according to strict bureaucratic principles.

Technological Development and the Trivialization of Science

If recent transformations in the techniques of research have led to an over-emphasis on method and therefore to the trivialization of the results of research, then one might expect that it would be the fields which have undergone such technical changes which would be the most trivialized. Unfortunately, there are no objective measures of the trivial or the redundant, and the arguments being examined often specify that the scientists themselves do not realize that their work is trivialized. On the other hand, this is one of the most highly publicized criticisms of contemporary science, and one might still wonder if differences between the disciplines in scientists' perceptions of these matters are associated with the differential use of modern techniques.

Considering that the new methods are said to reduce graduate education to narrow and inappropriate specialization, one might expect their differential use to be reflected in impressions of the adequacy of graduate education. For example, if a student specializes in his graduate advisors' techniques and instruments, he might probably realize the shortcomings of his education upon reaching his first post-graduate position. When Berelson questioned samples of recent Ph.D.'s precisely on this point, he found no difference between one scientific field and another (1960:202-203).

This result might well be due to differences between disciplines in the extent to which research has been trivialized. In fields where narrow focus and lack of insight have been fostered by the new methods, young scholars might not recognize their own inadequacies. Thus insofar as the trivialization of research and narrow specialization in graduate education are found together, one might not expect differences by field in the young scientists' assessments of their training.

But if the use of modern research techniques has brought about differences between the disciplines in the trivialization of research, one might suppose that there would be differences in older scientists' assessments of the intellectual vigor of their fields.[14] Berelson (1960:212) asked graduate faculty

---

[14]Klaw (1968:256-257) notes that many of the warnings that science is being subverted by changes summarized under the title "big science" have been voiced by elder statesmen of science. He attributes some of their apprehension to the tendency of older people to glorify the past and to suspect the present. Corroborative evidence

members in a variety of fields: "On the whole, how would you characterize the current state of health of your discipline nationally—in its intellectual vigor, development, progress, etc.?" He offered them response categories ranging from "very satisfactory" to "unsatisfactory" and reported the proportions who chose "very satisfactory" (Table 4-4).

Table 4-4.   Percent of Graduate Faculty Reporting the State of Their Discipline as "Very Satisfactory," by Discipline

Discipline	Percent
Physics	64%
Mathematics and Statistics	59%
Biology	49%
Chemistry	48%
Zoology	29%
Botany	25%
Sociology	21%
History	19%
English	10%
Political Science	6%

The six fields showing the highest levels of satisfaction in Table 4-4 are roughly comparable to the fields shown in Table 4-3: data for the subspecialties of chemistry and physics were not available to Berelson; "biology" is roughly comparable to Hagstrom's "experimental biology," and zoology and botany are but two members of Hagstrom's "other biology." Nevertheless, there is clearly little evidence of a negative association between the use of recently developed research methods as reported in Table 4-3, and satisfaction with the current state of the given field. For example, although in physics as a whole the new methods are in more common use than they are in mathematics and statistics, Table 4-4 shows physicists as the most satisfied. A similar reversal is revealed in the spokesmen of Hagstrom's "experimental biology" and "other biology."

Given the evidence cited above in footnote 14, one might wonder if differences in age could explain the results in Table 4-4. Berelson does not report age distributions in the various disciplines in his study of graduate faculty members, but Hagstrom (1967:112) presents data on the means and standard deviations of the dates on which his graduate faculty members obtained their Ph.D.'s. These measures correlate very highly with actual

has recently been presented by Ladd and Lipset (1972:1098), who report large differences between older and younger academic scientists' perceptions of the "soundness" of certain aspects of their professions, but only small differences between disciplines. For a comprehensive discussion of the correlates of age in science, see Zuckerman and Merton (1972).

chronological age, but differences between disciplines are quite small, and often in a direction opposite from what would be expected if the differences shown in Table 4-4 were simply a function of age composition (for example, those in "experimental biology" tend to be slightly older than those in "other biology"). It therefore seems unlikely that age composition can explain the large differences between the physical and natural sciences on the one hand, and the social sciences and humanities on the other.

Thus neither the results in Table 4-4, nor those concerning the recent Ph.Ds' judgments of the adequacy of their graduate education provide much support for the argument that the new methods routinize and trivialize research. Furthermore, the levels of satisfaction presented in Table 4-4 are not associated with modern forms of scientific teamwork as reported in Table 4-3.

Although the substantial variation among the fields in Table 4-4 is not easily explained by the argument that modern research techniques trivialize work, one might wonder if the variation perhaps reflects differences between fields in normative integration. This is not surprising since, as suggested in Chapter 2, scientists' opinions of their colleagues' work as "trivial" or "redundant," and the intellectual vigor of their fields can be taken to indicate consensus on the means and ends of research. If one also assumes that the development and use of new research instruments and techniques probably proceeds at a slower pace in sociology, history, English, and political science than in the other fields, then the results presented in Table 4-4 can be interpreted as consistent with the stand that lack of consensus on theoretical issues is shown in pessimism about a given field's intellectual vigor and a slow pace of development and exploitation of new research instruments and techniques. Thus, although the results presented in this section are cross-sectional rather than longitudinal, and are therefore not necessarily inconsistent with the argument that to take advantage of recently developed methods contributes to the intellectual disorganization of science, they are consistent with the view that routine in research and the use of modern techniques presuppose consensus on the ends and means of research.

As noted earlier, this does not imply strong positive correlations between scientific consensus, routine and the use of new techniques. In mathematics, for example, research workers may agree on definitions of appropriate research problems and of standards for determining if solutions have been reached, even though in their work there is not much routine. Optimism about the intellectual vigor of a field, on the part of both practitioners and outsiders, is related to the formers' perception of the possibility of providing definitive answers to important research problems.[15] Whether these answers can be obtained with the use of routine techniques appears to have no necessary relation to the belief that the problems are solvable.

---

[15]Edelstein has argued that the failure of Greek scientists to agree on the presuppositions and aims of the scientific enterprise contributed to ancient science's failure to become institutionalized (1963:27-33). Hagstrom (1965:187-222, 254-286) has outlined some of the mechanisms by which contemporary scientific communities deal with dissensus.

Conclusion

Although there seems to be sufficient evidence that research in fields with little consensus on theoretical issues is not greatly routinized, the preconditions of extensive routine are unknown. As a result, it seems unreasonable to assume a one-to-one correspondence between routine and normative integration.

Our attempts to assess the argument that associates routine in research with the trivialization of science, and that interprets both as a function of using complex and expensive techniques of modern research, have not yielded corroborative evidence. It is also true that the evidence is too weak to constitute a refutation, nevertheless, it seems unreasonable to conclude that the new methods have been important in determining routine in contemporary science. In Chapter 3 it was shown that research in mathematics and political science is less routine than in chemistry. The fact that routine is not associated with concern over the intellectual vigor and progress of the three fields (Table 4-4) would discourage the identification of the routinization of research with its trivialization.

These conclusions are consistent with arguments that some routine in research is not incompatible with scientific advance, and indeed, that the conditions which foster routine may also be particularly effective in making scientists aware that new and perhaps revolutionary departures from established perspectives are necessary for the attainment of a more adequate understanding of nature (Kuhn, 1963). In view of the inherent lack of routine in scientific research, it is doubtful whether the consequences of what routine does exist are analogous to the pathologies attributed to routine on the industrial assembly line.

POSTSCRIPT

The study of human work is intimately tied to questions of technological structure and to questions of "moral rule" (Hughes, 1951). Everyday work experiences are a function not only of the adequacy of tools, but also of the moral commitment of workers to their work and to the social structures in which it is performed. In the preceding chapters, I have presented an account of scientific research which touches on these two components of work experience. On the one hand, patterns of social solidarity define scientific communities within which scientists judge substantive questions of deviance, conformity, innovation, and stagnation. On the other hand, the relative routine of research in a given field is a function of the efficacy of the available mechanical and intellectual techniques. I have argued that many of the everyday experiences of research workers in a given field provide clues to the nature and strength of the social bonds which help unite their intellectual efforts, and to the technical bases of their research. On the basis of such clues, I have contrasted three scientific disciplines in terms of their patterns of social solidarity, and of the efficacy of their research techniques. In addition, I have attempted to evaluate a few popular hypotheses about the interrelation of the moral and technical orders of science by determining if some of their implications are reflected in differences between disciplines in the organization of research, and in scientists' satisfaction with their teaching and research.

Because research lies at the juncture of the moral and technical orders of science, it is possible to illuminate many of the concrete experiences of scientific life by means of a model of the social organization of the communities in which they occur. Having a paper rejected by a publisher, facing the necessity of coordinating one's efforts with those of colleagues in a research team, becoming anxious or depressed because work is not going forward—these are but a few of the experiences whose frequency varies widely from field to field and which may be interpreted as manifestations of differences in social organization. By attempting to interpret the research worker's everyday life in terms of the structure of the scientific community not only may his experiences be better understood, but better models may be attained for the analysis of the social structure of science.

APPENDIX

DESIGN AND EXECUTION OF THE STUDY

A. Sampling Procedures

The first and most important decision about sampling procedures in this study was to include a formal science, a physical science, and a social science. As indicated in Chapter 1, this was based on the need of an array of scientific fields showing large differences in patterns of work and social organization. Once the three specific fields were chosen, systematic random samples (Kish, 1967:113-123) were drawn from the directories of the American Chemical Society (1967) and the American Political Science Association (1968), and from faculty lists in the graduate school catalogues of universities offering the Ph.D. in mathematics (Mathematical Association of America, 1965). Previous studies of academic scientists using mailed questionnaires obtained response rates ranging from 40-70 percent, the variation being associated with the length of the questionnaire and the number of follow-ups required to induce members of the sample to return it. Since the questionnaire used in this study was only four pages long, and since two follow-up attempts were planned, response rates of approximately 70 percent were anticipated. Thus to obtain final samples of about 200 members each, original samples of 300 members were selected from each field.

Although these sampling lists were the best available for the populations to be studied, they did include a few scientists in fields other than those under study. Some departments of chemistry, for example, count in biochemists and chemical engineers as well as those in specialties traditionally identified as "chemistry"—analytical, physical, inorganic, and organic. Similarly, some departments of mathematics include statisticians while others do not. As a result it was necessary to screen out the biochemists and chemical engineers from chemistry, and the statisticians from mathematics, before the samples were finally selected.

The directory of political scientists included lists of those who identified themselves with several specialties; a single individual might identify himself with up to six specialties. In order to obtain a sample of political scientists whose work patterns were similar to those in other sciences, I sampled political scientists who claimed to belong in such specialties as political socialization, political parties and elections, and public opinion, and I did *not* sample those who identified themselves with such specialties as constitutional law, and normative political theory and philosophy. The outcome was a sample which overrepresents political scientists who carry out various types of empirical research, but does not exclude those interested in the last-named specialties.[1]

In the second week of April, 1969, questionnaires were sent to the 900 scientists in the three samples. Follow-up questionnaires were sent to non-respondents in early May and early June. In each sample circumstances, such as death, retirement and absence from the country excluded seven respondents (2½ percent). Of the remainder, 198 mathematicians (68 percent), 223 chemists (76 percent), and 217 political scientists (74 percent) returned completed or nearly completed questionnaires.

In order to check to what extent those who returned questionnaires represented the original samples, biographical data from standard sources such as *American Men of Science,* and information about scholarly publications from sources such as *Science Citation Index,* were collected for all in the original samples. Comparisons of the response rates of various categories within each field were then made, to find out if scientists in a particular category were over- or under-represented in the returns. For example, in order to check if those with various academic ranks had different response rates, response and rank were cross-classified. Beside academic rank, nine other variables were examined in this manner: respondent's year of doctorate, prestige of doctorate-granting institution, prestige of the institution where currently located, marital status, sex, number of articles published in 1968, number of times cited in 1968, specialty, and finally, whether the respondent held an administrative position such as department chairperson or dean, in 1969. Chi-square tests of association were carried out for 28 cross-classifications,[2] and seven of these 28 tests proved to be significant at the .20 alpha error level. Although it is clearly inappropriate to accept null hypotheses on the basis of such results, it is encouraging that the overall null hypothesis

---

[1] The political scientists overrepresented in the sample are sometimes characterized as "behaviorists." For a discussion of behaviorism in political science and a short description of its rise to dominance in American political science, see Pool (1967) and Almond (1967). For evidence and discussion of typical differences between more and less behavioralistically-inclined political scientists, see Somit and Tanenhaus (1964).

[2] Although there were ten possible cross-classifications in each field, and therefore 30 cross-classifications in all, it was impossible to construct two of them. The original sample of chemists included only two women and the cross-classification of response status by sex was therefore not constructed for chemistry. In addition, I did not have information about political scientists' primary specialties. Thus it was impossible to compare their response rates in different specialties in the same manner as was done in the case of mathematician and chemists.

(that these results are due to sampling error) was not rejected.[3] More important perhaps is the fact that in no case where a given variable had more than two ordered categories was there a monotonic relationship between its categories and response rates. Among mathematicians, those with doctorates from institutions of "medium prestige" were more likely to respond than were those from institutions either low or high in prestige, and those who published from one to three articles in 1968 were more likely to respond than if they had published either none or more than three; but among the remaining instances of statistically significant departures from independence, there were no cases even of such regular curvilinearities. Thus the evidence is that respondents are not unrepresentative of the original samples.

B. Measures of the Quantity and Quality of Scientific Productivity

The single most important technical development behind the recent growth of interest in the sociology of science has been the emergence of practical means to measure the quantity and quality of a scientist's published work. These measures have allowed research workers to undertake systematic investigation of a host of topics ranging from the determinants and correlates of productivity and eminence, to the relative impact of quantity and quality upon location in systems of academic stratification. Primarily responsible for the development of these measures is the *Science Citation Index* (SCI), which, since 1964, has provided research workers with counts of the number of scientific publications produced in a given year by a given writer, and of the number of times the writer's previous work is cited by others in that time (Institute for Scientific Information, 1968:7-10, 69-76). These two types of information correspond fairly well to common-sense notions of the "quantity" and "quality" of contributions to a discipline since they are based upon data gathered through its formal channels of communication. The counts of the publications and citations of men in my samples of mathematicians and chemists have been taken from the 1968 numbers of SCI.

The distributions of numbers of articles and citations in all three fields are highly positively skewed, and therefore I used the natural logarithms of the numbers (after adding a constant of 1.0 to accommodate those with no publications or citations) in order to transform their distributions into forms more nearly approximating normal distributions. The results involving these two variables are reported in this study in their transformed versions, but the correlations between the transformed and the untransformed versions tend to be high, and comparisons of results in each version reveal few differences as far as correlations with other variables are concerned.

Obtaining measures of the quantity and quality of a political scientist's work was more difficult than it was in the case of mathematicians and chemists for two reasons: first, political scientists were not included in references such as SCI and therefore alternate means of obtaining counts of publications and citations were needed; second, they are more likely than mathema-

---

[3]Since type-two rather than type-one error is at issue here, an alpha error-level larger than the customary .05 or .01 has been chosen. Using the normal curve as an approximation of the binomial distribution with P=.2 and N=28, one obtains a z-score of .66 for seven successes out of 28 independent trials.

ticians or chemists to present reports of their research in the form of books, thus necessitating a decision about the relative weighting of books and articles in any index of their productivity.

The first problem was met by selecting a sample of journals in which articles by political scientists are likely to appear, and then counting the number of articles that each member of my sample published in them, the number of citations of the previous work of each, and the number of their books which were reviewed in the journals. Of each journal the most current issues spanning one year were examined to make these three counts.[4]

In these efforts to make the measures of quantity and quality of work of political scientists as comparable as possible to the corresponding measures of mathematicians and chemists, two important sources of non-comparability should be noted. First, the journals which served as the sources of information concerning the political scientists do not form as comprehensive a sample of publications as those used by SCI. Thus it would be inappropriate to compare the three fields with respect to the overall rates of productivity of their members, and my data on the productivity of political scientists are probably more unreliable than those on mathematicians and chemists. Second, my enumeration of the citations of each political scientist include all such citations; they are not enumerations of the articles which cite a man's work, as is found in SCI. I decided to deviate from the procedure used by SCI because I needed large numbers of citations from each of the political science journals in order to carry out the analysis of citation patterns in them which is reported in Chapter 2.

Before deciding how to weight books and articles in an overall index of the productivity of political scientists, I examined the consequences of alternative strategies. Books are larger than articles and this fact apparently provides an *a priori* justification for giving them greater weight; among American sociologists, for example, according to Glenn and Villemez (1970:246), the practice of weighting books more than articles has widespread support. On the other hand, correlations between indices of productivity using weights from 1 to 3 for books (where 1 is the weight given an article) all range in the interval between .90 and 1.00. In addition, indices of productivity which give books higher weighting than articles have lower correlations with citations than does that index which gives books and articles equal weighting. For example, the correlation between citations and the index of productivity which gives books a weighting of 3 is .43, while the correlation between citations and the index which gives books an equal weighting with articles is .47. On the basis of this evidence, I decided to weight books and articles equally in my productivity index of political scientists.

---

[4]Ten journals were selected for this sample: the *American Political Science Review, World Politics, Comparative Political Studies, Journal of Politics, Western Political Quarterly, Political Science Quarterly, Public Opinion Quarterly, Administrative Science Quarterly, American Behavioral Scientist,* and *Foreign Affairs.* This list includes nearly all that political scientists identify as key journals in their field (Somit and Tanenhaus, 1964:86-92). In addition, I included the 1967 issues of *American Political Science Review.*

REFERENCES

Almond, Gabriel A.
    1967   "Political theory and political science." Pp. 1-21 in Ithiel de Sola Pool (ed.),
          Contemporary Political Science: Toward Empirical Theory. New York:
          McGraw-Hill.
American Chemical Society
    1967   Directory of Graduate Research. Washington, D.C.: American Chemical
          Society.
American Mathematical Society
    1969   Combined Membership List 1969-70. Providence, Rhode Island: American
          Mathematical Society.
American Political Science Association
    1968   Biographical Directory 1968. Washington, D.C.: The Goetz Co.
Barber, Bernard
    1962   Science and the Social Order. New York: Collier.
Ben David, Joseph
    1960   "Scientific productivity and academic organization in nineteenth century
          medicine." American Sociological Review 25(December):828-43.
    1964   "Scientific growth: a sociological view." Minerva 2(Summer):455-76.
Berelson, Bernard
    1960   Graduate Education in the United States. New York: McGraw-Hill.
Blauner, Robert
    1964   Alienation and Freedom: The Factory Worker and His Industry. Chicago:
          University of Chicago Press.
Bochner, Salomon
    1963   "Revolutions in physics and crises in mathematics." Science 141(2
          August):408-11.

Brown, David G.
    1967   The Mobile Professors. Washington, D.C.: American Council on Education.

Cole, Stephen and Jonathan R. Cole
    1967   "Scientific output and recognition: a study in the operation of the reward system in science." American Sociological Review 32(June):377-90.
    1968   "Visibility and the structural bases of awareness of scientific research." American Sociological Review 33(June):397-413.

Collins, Randall
    1968   "Competition and social control in science: an essay in theory construction." Sociology of Education 41(Spring):123-40.

Committee for the Survey of Chemistry
    1965   Chemistry: Opportunities and Needs. Washington, D.C.: National Academy of Sciences.

Crane, Diana
    1965   "Scientists at major and minor universities: a study of productivity and recognition." American Sociological Review 30(October):699-714.
    1972   Invisible Colleges: Diffusion of Knowledge in Scientific Communities. Chicago, Illinois: University of Chicago Press.

Downey, Kenneth J.
    1969   "The scientific community: organic or mechanical." Sociological Quarterly 10(Fall):438-54.

Dubin, Robert
    1956   "Industrial workers' worlds: a study of the 'central life interests' of the industrial workers." Social Problems 3(January):131-42.

Duncan, O.D., R.P. Cuzzort and B. Duncan
    1961   Statistical Geography. Glencoe, Illinois: Free Press.

Durkheim, Emile
    1947   The Division of Labor in Society. Trans. by George Simpson. Glencoe, Illinois: Free Press.
    1951   Suicide. Trans. by John A. Spaulding and George Simpson. New York: Free Press.

Edelstein, Ludwig
    1963   "Motives and incentives for science in antiquity." Pp. 15-41 in A.C. Crombie (ed.), Scientific Change. New York: Basic Books.

Feigl, Herbert
    1953   "The scientific outlook: naturalism and humanism." Pp. 8-18 in Herbert Feigl and May Brodbeck (eds.), Readings in the Philosophy of Science. New York: Appleton-Century-Crofts.

Fisher, Charles S.
    1967   "The last invariant theorists: a sociological study of the collective biographies of mathematical specialists." European Journal of Sociology 8(No. 2): 216-44.
    1973   "Some social characteristics of mathematicians and their work." American Journal of Sociology 78(March):1094-1118.

Gamow, George
    1966   Thirty Years that Shook Physics. Garden City, New York: Doubleday.

Garfinkel, Harold
    1964   "Studies of the routine grounds of everyday activities." Social Problems 11(Winter):225-50.

Garvey, William D., Nan Lin and Carnot E. Nelson
1970 "Some comparisons of communication activities in the physical and social sciences." Pp. 61-84 in Carnot E. Nelson and D.K. Pollock (eds.), Communication Among Scientists and Engineers. Lexington, Massachusetts: D.C. Heath and Co.

Gaston, Jerry
1973 Originality and Competition in Science. Chicago, Illinois: University of Chicago Press.

Glaser, Barney G.
1964 Organizational Scientists: Their Professional Careers. Indianapolis, Indiana: Bobbs-Merrill.

Glenn, Norval D. and Wayne Villemez
1970 "The productivity of sociologists at 45 American universities." The American Sociologist 5(August):244-52.

Guttman, Louis
1953 "Image theory for the structure of quantitative variates." Psychometrica 18(December):277-96.

Hadamard, Jacques
1954 The Psychology of Invention in the Mathematical Field. New York: Dover.

Hagstrom, Warren O.
1964a "Anomy in scientific communities." Social Problems 12(Fall):186-95.
1964b "Traditional and modern forms of scientific teamwork." Administrative Science Quarterly 9(December):241-63.
1965 The Scientific Community. New York: Basic Books.
1967 Competition and teamwork in science. Madison, Wisconsin: Final Report to the National Science Foundation
1970 "Factors related to the use of different modes of publishing research in four scientific fields." Pp. 85-124 in Carnot E. Nelson and D.K. Pollock (eds.), Communication Among Scientists and Engineers. Lexington, Massachusetts: D.C. Heath and Co.

Hargens, Lowell L. and Warren O. Hagstrom
1967 "Sponsored and contest mobility of American academic scientists." Sociology of Education 40(Winter):24-38.

Harmon, Harry H.
1960 Modern Factor Analysis. Chicago, Illinois: University of Chicago Press.

Hastorf, A.H., D.J. Schneider and J. Polefka
1970 Person Perception. Reading, Massachusetts: Addison-Wesley.

Hempel, Carl G.
1965 Aspects of Scientific Explanation. New York: Free Press.

Hudson, L. and B. Jacot
1971 "Marriage and fertility in academic life." Nature 229(19 February):531-32.

Hughes, Everett C.
1951 "Mistakes at work." Canadian Journal of Economics and Political Science 17(August):320-27.

Institute for Scientific Information
1968 Science Citation Index 1968 Guide and Journal Lists. Philadelphia, Pennsylvania: Institute for Scientific Information.

Kish, Leslie
1967 Survey Sampling. New York: Wiley.

Klaw, Spencer
1968   The New Brahims: Scientific Life in America. New York: William Morrow and Co.

Kuhn, Thomas S.
1961   "The function of measurement in modern physical science." Pp. 31-63 in Harry Woolf (ed.), Quantification: A History of the Meaning of Measurement in the Natural and Social Sciences. Indianapolis, Indiana: Bobbs-Merrill.
1962   The Structure of Scientific Revolutions. Chicago, Illinois: University of
and   Chicago Press.
1970a   (2nd Ed.)
1963   "The essential tension: tradition and innovation in scientific research." Pp. 341-54 in C.W. Taylor and F. Barron (eds.), Scientific Creativity: Its Recognition and Development. New York: Wiley.
1970b   "Reflections on my critics." Pp. 231-78 in I. Lakatos and A. Musgrave (eds.), Criticism and the Growth of Knowledge. Cambridge: Cambridge University Press.

Ladd, E.C., Jr. and S.M. Lipset
1972   "Politics of natural scientists and engineers." Science 176(June):1091-98.

Landecker, Werner S.
1951   "Types of integration and their measurement." American Journal of Sociology 56(January):332-40.

Litwak, Eugene
1961   "Models of bureaucracy which permit conflict." American Journal of Sociology 67(September):177-84.

Lodahl, Janice B. and Gerald Gordon
1972   "The structure of scientific fields and the functioning of university graduate departments." American Sociological Review 37(February):57-72.

Mannheim, Karl
1940   Man and Society in an Age of Reconstruction. New York: Harcourt, Brace and World.

Mansfield, Harvey C.
1962   "Toward a definition of editorial policy for the Review." American Political Science Review 56(March):129-38.

Masterman, Margaret
1970   "The nature of a paradigm." Pp. 59-89 in I. Lakatos and A. Musgrave (eds.), Criticism and the Growth of Knowledge. Cambridge: Cambridge University Press.

Mathematical Association of America
1965   Guidebook to Departments in the Mathematical Sciences in the United States and Canada. Buffalo, New York: Mathematical Association of America.

Marx, Karl
1964   Selected Writings in Sociology and Social Psychology. Trans. by T.B. Bottomore. New York: McGraw-Hill.

Merton, Robert K.
1934   "Durkheim's Division of Labor in Society." American Journal of Sociology 40(November):319-28.
1957a   Social Theory and Social Structure. Glencoe, Illinois: Free Press.
1957b   "Priorities in scientific discovery: a chapter in the sociology of science." American Sociological Review 22(December):635-59.

1965 "The ambivalence of scientists." Pp. 112-32 in Norman Kaplan (ed.), Science and Society. Chicago, Illinois: Rand McNally.

1967 Abstract of "The Matthew effect in the rewarding and communication structure of science." Abstracts of the 62nd Annual Meeting of the American Sociological Association :98.

1968 "The Matthew effect in science." Science 159(5 January):56-63.

Mullins, Nicholas C.
1968 "The distribution of social and cultural properties in informal communication networks among biological scientists." American Sociological Review 33(October):786-97.

National Science Foundation, Office of Science Information Service
1964 Characteristics of Scientific Journals, 1949-1959. Washington, D.C.: National Science Foundation.

Nisbet, Robert A.
1965 Emile Durkheim. Englewood Cliffs, New Jersey: Prentice-Hall.

Parsons, Talcott
1951 The Social System. Glencoe, Illinois: Free Press.

Perrow, Charles
1967 "A framework for the comparative analysis of organizations." American Sociological Review 32(April):194-208.

Polanyi, Michael
1955 "Pure and applied science and their appropriate forms of organization." Pp. 39-49 in Congress of Cultural Freedom, Science and Freedom. London: Martin Secker and Warburg, Ltd.

Pool, Ithiel de Sola
1967 "Forward." Pp. V-XIII in Ithiel de Sola Pool (ed.), Contemporary Political Science: Toward Empirical Theory. New York: McGraw-Hill.

Popper, Karl
1970 "Normal science and its dangers." Pp. 51-58 in I. Lakatos and A. Musgrave (eds.), Criticism and the Growth of Knowledge. Cambridge: Cambridge University Press.

Price, Derek J. de Solla
1965a Little Science, Big Science. New York: Columbia University Press.

1965b "Networks of scientific papers." Science 149(30 July):510-15.

1970 "Citation measures of hard science, soft science, technology, and non-science." Pp. 3-22 in Carnot E. Nelson and D.K. Pollock (eds.), Communication Among Scientists and Engineers. Lexington, Massachusetts: D.C. Heath and Co.

Ranney, Austin
1969 "Procedures for reviewing manuscripts." American Political Science Review 63(March):168-69.

Roe, Anne
1953 "A psychological study of eminent psychologists and anthropologists, and a comparison with biological and physical scientists." Psychological Monographs 67(No. 352).

Ryder, Norman B.
1968 "Report of the editor of the American Sociological Review." The American Sociologist 3(November):331.

Scheff Thomas J.
1967 "Toward a sociological model of consensus." American Sociological Review 32(February):32-46.

Schwartz, M. and C.G. Schwartz
    1955   "Problems in participant observation." American Journal of Sociology 60(January):343-53.

Seeman, Melvin
    1966   "Report of the editor of *Sociometry*." The American Sociologist 1(November):284-85.

Selvin, Hanan C. and Alan Stuart
    1966   "Data-dredging procedures in survey analysis." The American Statistician 20(June):20-23.

Shapere, Dudley
    1971   "The paradigm concept." Science 172(14 May):706-9.

Sjoberg, G.
    1967   Ethics, Politics, and Social Research. Cambridge, Massachusetts: Schenkman.

Somit, Albert and Joseph Tanenhaus
    1964   American Political Science: A Profile of a Discipline. New York: Atherton Press.

Stinchcombe, Arthur L.
    1966   "On getting 'hung-up' and other assorted illnesses." The Johns Hopkins Magazine (Winter):25-30.

Storer, Norman W.
    1966   The Social System of Science. New York: Holt, Rinehart and Winston.
    1967   "The hard sciences and the soft: some sociological observations." Bulletin of the Medical Library Association 55(January):75-84.
    1972   "Relations among scientific disciplines." Pp. 229-68 in S. Nagi and R. Corwin (eds.), The Social Contexts of Research. New York: Wiley.

Swatez, Gerald M.
    1970   "The social organization of a university laboratory." Minerva 8(January): 36-58.

Taeuber, Karl E. and Alma F. Taeuber
    1965   Negroes in Cities. Chicago, Illinois: Aldine.

Walker, Charles R. and Robert H. Guest
    1952   The Man on the Assembly Line. Cambridge, Massachusetts: Harvard University Press.

Webb, Eugene, Donald T. Campbell, Richard D. Schwartz and Lee Sechrest
    1966   Unobtrusive Measures. Chicago, Illinois: Rand McNally.

Weber, Max
    1946   "Science as a vocation." Pp. 129-56 in H.H. Gerth and C.W. Mills (eds. and trans.), From Max Weber: Essays in Sociology. New York: Oxford University Press.

Weiss, Paul A.
    1971   Within the Gates of Science and Beyond: Science and Its Cultural Commitments. New York: Hefner.

Whyte, William H. Jr.
    1956   The Organization Man. Garden City, New York: Doubleday.

Wilson, Kenneth M.
    1965   Of Time and the Doctorate. Atlanta, Georgia: Southern Regional Education Board.

Zetterberg, Hans L.
    1967   "Scientific acedia." Sociological Focus 1(Fall):1-11.

Zuckerman, Harriet and Robert K. Merton

1971 ''Patterns of evaluation in science: institutionalization, structure and functions of the referee system.'' Minerva 9(January):66-100.

1972 ''Age, aging, and age structure in science.'' Pp. 292-356 in Matilda W. Riley et al. (eds.), Aging and Society. New York: Russell Sage.